Under the Jolly Roger

British Submariners At War 1939 - 1945

by
Dave J. Quigley

First published 1988

Published by Portsmouth Publishing and Printing Ltd.,
The News Centre, Military Road,
Hilsea, Portsmouth, Hants. PO2 9SX

Typeset at The News Centre, Portsmouth

Make-up by Steve Walker

Cover design by Ian Shepherd

Printed by Conifer Press, Fareham

ISBN 1 871182 03 4

Contents

DEDICATION

This book is dedicated to the memory of all submariners of World War II who served their mother country with bravery, fortitude and dedication. It is to them and others like them in the Armed Forces of our country that we owe our freedom and lifestyle of today.

"LEST WE FORGET"

Author's introduction

Much has been written about submarines during the Second World War, some of it from official sources, some from the memory of those involved, and some, propaganda-type stories, which are almost pure fiction. This book is an attempt to put down in print stories, songs and poems which are all the work of men who served in British submarines between 1939-45.

Many of them are written down as told some 40 years after the event, and there may well be occasional factual data which is not historically correct. Some of the originators are no longer with us, and with the passing years the number of survivors is getting fewer and fewer. It was with this thought in mind that I decided to prepare this book. Many of the stories contained in it have been picked up as a by-product of research that I have been doing in the archives of the Royal Navy Submarine Museum at Gosport.

Today we tend to think of a submarine as a very complex high technology weapons system, which, of course, it certainly is. In fact it is probably the most sophisticated weapon in use in the arsenals of today. In the days of World War II, this was not the case. They had little in the way of navigation equipment and even less of a weapons control system. The success with which they operated must be put down to the skill and bravery of the men who served in them.

It is intended that this book serve as a memorial to all who served in submarines, not only to those who died in the defence of their country but to all without whose dedication and skill the exploits that make up the history of the submarine service would not have happened.

I wish to thank a large number of people, too many to mention all by name, but special mention should be made of the help and encouragement given to me by Gus Britton, Deputy Director of the Submarine Museum, and Ray Gritt, editor of the Submarine Old Comrades Association Newsletter, who have both given me an almost free hand in the use of material from their archives. To everyone else who has contributed stories, I thank you most sincerely. Without your help this volume would not have been possible.

If any reader has a similar story that he would like considered for publication, it is my intention to prepare a second volume, and I would be only too pleased to receive it.

Dave J. Quigley,
Cowes, Isle of Wight

Foreword

By Captain J.S. Stevens, D.S.O., D.S.C., R.N. (Retd.)

This book is a collection of memories of submariners, mainly during World War II, in their own unofficial language. Nearly all the contributors are chief petty officers, petty officers and junior ratings. Many tell what happened when one of our submarines was sunk and there were survivors. They reveal many selfless acts of individuals helping others to safety.

"Round Trip" describes the exploits of E.R.A.s Hammond and Lister, who became prisoners-of-war after H.M. Submarine *Shark* was sunk off south-west Norway in July, 1940. After being held in various camps, including Colditz – rare for ratings – they became the only R.N. submariners to escape and get back to the U.K., via Switzerland, Gibraltar and other places, while the war was on.

"P39 and Olympus," by W.G. Wright, C.E.R.A., describes how, after nearly four years overseas in four submarines, he married, then stood by P39 completing at Vickers, Barrow. After a few patrols from Malta in 1941, she was sunk in harbour by the Luftwaffe. He then joined *Olympus* for passage to U.K., but she sank in nine minutes after striking a mine in the swept channel exiting Malta. He was one of nine survivors out of more than 90 on board who succeeded in swimming seven miles ashore to Malta in a sea temperature of 52 degrees. He had never swum more than half a mile before. He then took passage back to U.K. in a fast surface minelayer and went to Barrow again to stand by *Tactician,* completing in 1942. He served in her for two years in the Mediterranean and Far East with plenty of action. One man's war. . . . .what a war!

I must mention "Timoshenko" by Joe Lewis, P.O. Tel. I was C.O. of *Unruffled* in 1942-43 while this cat was on board. He received a fair amount of publicity in the British Press as the cat who strongly disapproved of enemy activity such as depth charge attacks. I can testify that he was a morale-raiser; near panic used to appear if he could not be found shortly before sailing on a patrol.

Older submariners will want to buy, scrounge or steal a copy of this book, and naval historians, as well as the general public, will also want it.

The loss of H.M. Submarine Starfish

by M. Bowra

All the months of tedious practice would now be put to the test. The skipper made his intentions clear – we were going to attack. Torpedo tubes were made ready and slowly and deliberately *Starfish* was brought into the attack position, the distance between herself and the target reducing with every second that passed. Donald held his breath. This was the closest he had been to action.

Unknown to *Starfish* the enemy vessel had already detected them and was closing in for an attack of her own. Lieut. Turner's voice broke the silence as he muttered: "We can't miss" and gave the orders to despatch our cargo of torpedoes.

"Fire One, Fire Two, Fire Three, Fire Four!"

The enemy was at 500 yards and moving at 19 knots, its progress being constantly monitored by the hydrophone operators, Harry Shipp and Wilkens. Turner barked out his next order: "Sixty feet, steer 270" but he already knew something was wrong. With all the weight of the torpedoes leaving the boat the trim should have altered considerably, but it hadn't. Turner looked at Ldg. Tel. Shipp on the hydrophones, but a negative response compounded his fears. No torpedoes were on their way to the target – a target that was now homing in on them. Turner's worst fears were realised when almost immediately P.O. Clarke, the TGM, reported that he had not received the order to fire the torpedoes. Turner's stream of abuse turned the air blue within the control room. After all the practice and drill, they had fouled up the procedure through a misunderstanding of message passing. Turner, still fuming, decided to come to periscope depth to ascertain if another attack was possible. Meanwhile, above, the enemy vessel had stopped and was searching for her prey, oblivious to the fact that she herself had just escaped destruction.

Turner checked with his hydrophone operators and after receiving the all-clear brought the periscope up to break the surface. With his cap turned back to front and tilted to the back of his head, he scanned the area where he expected the enemy to be. Nothing. Swearing slightly under his breath, he rotated the periscope through 360 degrees and was confronted by the enemy vessel, which filled the lens of the periscope. A minesweeper, not a destroyer as at first thought, was lying stopped only about 70 yards away. Turner swore again, but this time louder, realising that his boat was now in a position of extreme danger. He immediately ordered *Starfish* to 60 feet. The German minesweeper had seen the tell-tale sign of the periscope and closed in for the kill. Within a few seconds two depth charges were despatched, but did not explode.

The sudden change in direction of *Starfish* and the angry words coming from the control room made Donald realise that all was not well. The distinct sound of propellers above and two loud splashes outside the hull of the boat confirmed his anxiety. Donald steadied himself against the casing of one of the diesels, waiting for the explosion that would surely come. He felt *Starfish* lurch to one side and then the angle of the deck began to increase. He didn't know if the depth charges had gone off or not but what he was sure of was that the boat was now coming up. His emotions changed dramatically, excitement replaced by fear.

Starfish had lost power to her fore hydroplanes and was starting to come up bows first. Turner took the only course of action open to him and quickly ordered all tanks to be flooded. The angle of the deck slowly levelled off and *Starfish* began her descent to the bottom. As the submarine jolted to a stop on the seabed, the crew received the order for total silence. Everybody knew the reason. The Germans would be equipped with powerful listening devices, scanning the area for the slightest sound that would lead them to their target. Even a cough or a spanner dropped would mean almost certain detection. Donald settled back into the most comfortable position he could find and removed his boots as ordered.

The silence within the boat was almost unbearable and the atmosphere could have been cut with a knife – 39 men motionless and silent, waiting and praying that they would not be found. As *Starfish* lay on the seabed, almost like a tomb, the minesweeper criss-crossed above tirelessly in an effort to make contact with her target. Roles had now been reversed, the hunter had become the hunted.

An hour passed agonisingly, and the only sound in the boat was that of whispered voices and men breathing heavily. Donald tried to let his mind go blank and not dwell on his immediate predicament, but no matter how hard he tried his mind kept wandering back to the same thing. An image of Evelyn reading a postcard stating that he was lost, presumed dead. His mouth was dry and although the temperature within the boat was dropping he had to wipe sweat from his brow. He glanced momentarily at the others huddled about him and saw one emotion on their faces, fear. He felt slightly comforted that he was not alone in his feelings. Only a fool could possibly enjoy this experience and it was certainly not exciting any more. At any time the bulkheads could come caving in, bringing a terrible, horrific death. All Donald wanted to hear was the voice of Lieut. Turner, ordering the main motors started so that they could get the hell out of it. As each minute passed without the command so Donald's nerves became more on edge.

Donald checked his watch once more. 10.50. He could hardly believe his eyes. They had been bottomed for just over an hour but it seemed like a lifetime. He was just about to shake his watch to make sure it was still working when a muffled voice interrupted. The order had been given to start up one of the compass motors. To Donald that

Petty Officer Donald Bowra, whose son, Michael, is the author of this chapter, which graphically describes his father's experience in H.M. Submarine Starfish.

could mean only one thing – the Skipper intended to go somewhere. He had barely began to tell Taffy, sitting alongside him, that one of the Sperry motors had started up when the boat was rocked violently by several loud, external explosions. This time they were close. Light bulbs shattered in their sockets and showered fragments over the crouching figures, and several high pressure air lines split, adding to the confusion. Debris of every description littered the boat and amongst it lay the dazed and shaken crewmen.

Donald's head felt as if it was coming apart at the seams, and all he could hear was a loud ringing in his ears. He tried to focus his eyes on the scene around him but it was just a haze. People were shouting but he could not hear them. From somewhere water was gushing into the boat and was mixing with the lubricating oil that was also bubbling on to the deck casing. Slowly his senses returned to normal. Frenzied activity was going on throughout the boat, with desperate attempts to stop the flow of oil and water. Everywhere men were to be seen heaving on wrenches, working now in total silence. Slowly and surely the situation was brought under control. Some of the repairs were crude but they worked. The whole submarine looked in a terrible state and the men were exhausted from their exertions. Donald did not have to be told that *Starfish* could not stand up to many more attacks like that.

For the moment the submarine was out of danger and the crew settled back to take a well-earned rest, listen and wait. Another hour passed, to many the longest in their lives. In the distance could be heard the ominous sound of the minesweeper's propellers as she swished through the cold dark waters of the Heligoland Bight, sometimes loud and sometimes getting fainter, only to return once more. To Donald they seemed to be a long way off and his hopes began to rise that they had lost contact. This was dashed at mid-day, when out of the blue several depth charges exploded in the near vicinity of the submarine and sent debris crashing once more on to the crouching frightened men.

Lieut. Turner decided to remain bottomed. If they moved they would surely be detected on the German's hydrophones. At present they appeared to be dropping their charges at random and a slim chance of evading the closing net existed. Two more long and tedious hours passed with still no sign that the minesweeper above had located the exact position of *Starfish.* The submarine had been motionless for more than five hours, and in all that time the crew had sat still and quiet.

The pressure was starting to tell on their faces as many just stared into space or at their feet. Many constantly fidgeted with their clothing or hands. Donald had allowed his mind to drift back to the days when he worked at the Cosmo, but it seemed a lifetime ago. He was both frightened and angry at the same time. Twenty-three years of age with so much in front of him, only to die at the hand of people he had never seen. Again his thoughts went back to Evelyn – she would never know what had really happened to him. His melancholy mood was rudely interrupted by the sound of a straining voice cursing and swearing. One of the crewmen had been forced to answer the call of nature, but with the heads out of operation had squatted on a bucket. Somehow, the thought of the poor unfortunate going through the motions, whilst the German Navy roamed about above, amused Donald. He wondered if the disgusting sounds could be heard on the listening devices. The thought must have occurred to someone else, because an angry whispered voice encouraged the man to put a cork up his rear end.

Donald wiped the sweat from his brow with an oily rag that he carried in his overall pocket. The temperature within the boat had continued to drop steadily, but there was no way he could stop the beads of perspiration forming on his skin. He tried in vain to put all thoughts of death out of his mind, reasoning that the officers in charge of *Starfish* appeared to know what they were doing and could probably be relied upon to make the right decisions. His thoughts were rudely shattered by an eerie pinging noise that grew louder and faster. The sound was coming from outside the boat. Donald knew what it was. The Germans had a similar detection system to the Royal Navy's ASDIC, and were searching and getting closer by the minute. In the far distance came the faint sound of propellers churning through the water and there was no mistaking that the noise was getting stronger. He listened intently, his gaze for some reason directed straight up, almost as if expected to see his hunters. They were not turning away as before but heading straight for the submarine's position. Almost in despair he swore gently under his breath: "The bastards have found us."

Donald felt every one of his muscles go tense and held his breath in anticipation of what must surely come. Like the sound of an express train thundering through a station, the minesweeper swept directly overhead, its propellers whipping the sea into a frenzy. Donald was

H.M. Submarine Starfish, depth-charged and sunk in the Heligoland Bight on January 20, 1940. Her crew survived to be taken prisoner-of-war.

sure that he heard two distinct clicks, and then all hell was let loose. Ten depth charges exploded in close proximity to the dormant submarine. If the men thought they had lived through the worst, they were badly mistaken. Again light bulbs exploded in their sockets, plunging the boat into near total darkness. Water and high pressure air streamed into the stricken submarine, adding to the panic.

Donald, clutching his head in his hands could not believe the sight in front of him. In the murky light, several of the boat's hull plates appeared to spring apart from the force of the explosion and then return to their original position. Before he could move, several heavy duty rivets were torn from their holes and ricocheted off the engine casing, beside his head. Men were shouting and screaming, trying desperately to stem the leaks of oil, water, and air. Slowly, and with great credit to the engineering department, the situation was brought under control. Just when it looked as though the men had won their battle, ten more charges dropped into the sea above *Starfish*.

One of the large, brass ship's clocks came flying off the wall, narrowly missing Donald's head, and smashed against the opposite casing. Again a rivet, as though fired from a gun, careered across the boat and rebounded off the starboard diesel. Another explosion this time sent Donald hurtling into Russell, who was alongside him, and together they crashed to the deck. Pieces of glass and metal showered down on top of them. As they fought to get back up, the submarine rocked again as though it was just a cork. A member of the crew who was just a blur to Donald leapt over him as he grovelled on the floor. Donald noticed the damp patch on his trousers – he had wet himself, but who could blame him.

Again another explosion threatened to rip the boat apart. Donald's vision was now totally blurred and his nerves were at breaking point. Men were shouting and cursing and trying to prevent themselves from being thrown around. A large jet of steam was flashing from one of the split pipes and resisted all attempts to stop it. A couple of men had vomited and the mess floated lazily in the water covering the deck. Donald clutched his head and tried to clear his brain. He was attempting to tighten a flange on the fuel line, but his strength seemed to have evaporated. Russell gave him a hand and together they were able to move the wrench and manage to tighten the joint. Donald went to smile, but another explosion spun him round and he was sent flying into the diesel again.

This time he was sure of what he had seen. Some of the pressure plates had sprung open and returned due to the tremendous force exerted upon them. They had to stop the leaks or perish. Donald was soaked to the skin, both with sweat and water. His face was covered in oil and grease and spatters of blood trickled from his ears and nose. Dodsworth was shouting orders to everyone, and desperately trying to discover where all the water and oil was coming from. Donald expected at any moment for the hull to split open and thousands of gallons of water to come rushing in. There seemed no way out. Every time they repaired one leak another took its place. They were fighting a battle that the sea outside looked certain to win.

Donald heard the loud click outside the boat once again, and this time he threw himself to the deck. He was just in time, as another charge exploded right above the submarine. There wasn't much else to come off the walls, but a rivet missed his head by a couple of inches. He finally snapped and shouted at the top of his voice, but his abuse was drowned amongst the noise being generated within the boat.

The whole boat now resembled a shower house. From every conceivable position water spurted or air hissed. Dodsworth and his team worked feverishly, using every method possible to prevent the boat from becoming just another wreck on the sea floor. The fore ends had suffered the worst, and Donald heard from some of the seamen that she was split open. He knew that this submarine would not be going very far and the realisation that *Starfish* would probably never return to the surface dawned upon him. Working tirelessly, wherever help was needed, Donald was becoming demoralised. It seemed a hopeless task, but amongst all the confusion, one man stood out as he relentlessly pushed seamen and stokers into specific tasks. Engine Room Artificer Stan Cook, but he, too, was fighting a losing battle to save *Starfish.*

Their situation was now becoming desperate. A message was passed from the control room for blocks and tackle. Both the gun and conning tower hatches had lifted and sprung leaks. Spare light bulbs had, by this time, been fitted and they illuminated a grisly scene. The compartments looked as though a maniac had run amok with a sledgehammer, determined to wreak as much damage as possible. The tired and mentally exhausted crewmen were nearly at the end of their tether as they worked in atrocious conditions to repair the damage. Some were up to their waists in a mixture of freezing water and lubricating oil. Water was still seeping into the boat from numerous places and was washing along the metal deck plates. The toilet bucket that had given Donald a moment of amusement had been upturned in the confusion, and its nauseating contents now joined the other debris floating in the water.

Again, the men brought the submarine back to some sort of normality. The skipper, obviously worried about the deteriorating state of his boat, called for a damage report. Dodsworth, accompanied by Stan Cook, entered the engine room and started to take stock. Donald looked at the E.R.A. and asked the question that everybody wanted to know. Stan Cook shrugged his shoulders and with a weak, tired smile gave his answer: "Always a chance, always." With that he patted Donald on the back and ducked through the hatch leading back into the control room. Lieut. Turner scanned the various damage reports in front of him, shaking his head slowly.

Fifty per cent. of light out of action.
Numerous leaks in the pressure hull due to loose rivets.
Isolated leaks due to partial opening of seams in the hull.
High pressure air lines fractured in several places.
Aft bulkhead buckled and distorted in torpedo room.
Rivets sheared and shell plating sprung.
Oil fuel filling pipe sheared.
Serious damage to hull beneath lubricating tanks in engine room.
Engine crank cases flooded.
Leakage through tank tops.
Starboard main motor bearing flooded.

Petty Officer Donald Bowra at a reunion of the crew of the submarine Seal at the village of Seal, in Kent. Villagers "adopted" the boat at the beginning of the war, and Donald Bowra came to know many of Seal's crew when they were prisoners-of-war together.

In plain terms, *Starfish* was in a state. She was leaking badly in the fore-ends and one main engine at least was inoperative. There was nothing that could be done to stem the flow of water into the fore-ends, so reluctantly Turner ordered the area to be evacuated and shut off. The men present in the control room knew only too well what that meant. With the bows flooded, it would act like a dead weight if ever the submarine tried to surface.

The time now was 1600. The men were cold, tired, hungry and dispirited, the majority not only physically exhausted but mentally drained as well. Donald's head was still spinning and he felt as though he was suffering from the worst hangover of his life. The skipper, mindful of the morale of his crew, decided to take a chance and ordered hot soup to be served. The only comfort to him was that sea water had not yet reached the batteries and their deadly acid. If that happened their days were numbered. Deadly chlorine gas would quickly mix with the already stale air and deliver the men to a ghastly death. He knew, however, that *Starfish* could not survive another close attack and he ordered the confidential books and signals to be destroyed.

The stench of sweat, fuel oil, rotting food, urine and excrement tainted still further the stale and musty air within the boat, making normal breathing unpleasant. Dodsworth entered the engine room with the documents to be destroyed. Stoker Les Wear tipped several old potatoes out of a bucket and offered the receptacle to the Engineer Officer. With the burning paper, soaked in engine oil, adding to the smells in the engine compartment, Donald found he was inhaling deeper and harder as the time slipped slowly by.

Again came the noise they all feared. The water above was being disturbed by the propellers of a ship. They had returned again. This time the vessel, unlike previous occasions, stopped directly overhead. The men held their breath but nothing happened. The suspense was unbearable. Donald wanted to shout out. Tell them to get on with it. The sound started up again and moved away. Donald breathed low and hard and turned to Russell.

"Perhaps they have lost us."

Russell shook his head and replied softly, almost as if he was talking to himself, "No chance."

All was quiet again and the men returned to their repairs, trying desperately to keep the noise to a minimum. Again the ship passed overhead, but this time closely followed by another. Reinforcements. Still no more depth charges were dropped. Unbeknown to the men in the submarine, after one of the heavy attacks a large air bubble was observed breaking the surface, obviously coming from the stricken boat below. The Germans had marked the spot with lighted buoys and were now content to sit and wait. They knew that eventually the air would run out and the submarine would have to surface, if it was able.

By 1800 the situation in the boat had deteriorated badly. All of the bilges were now full of water, the engine room crank cases and starboard motor bearings were also flooded. Sea water was seeping into the lubricating tanks and water was also pouring into the boat through the starboard clutch and lapping against the motor casing. The atmosphere was getting worse by the minute and the crew grew more lethargic.

Lieut. Turner had another agonising decision to make. If they remained bottomed for much longer, they would never make it back to the surface. He knew that the enemy were somewhere in the vicinity, so his original plan of slipping away after dark was now looking out of the question, unless they had a great deal of luck. Donald and the rest of the crew only wanted one thing: to get this scrapheap off the bottom and back to where they thought they might stand some chance of survival.

The order was given to issue the Davis escape gear. As padlocks and seals were being broken, Donald's mind drifted back to the conversation he had had back at Blockhouse.

"Only good for shallow water."

Donald reflected that surely they must be O.K. in 90 feet. When the kits were handed out it was found that several of them were useless as the rubber hoses had perished. Donald decided that he would use one only if totally necessary. The boat had gone quiet again, everybody waiting impatiently for the order to be given. At 1820 it came.

"Prepare to surface."

The sound of rushing air tore through the boat and seemed to go on for ever. Donald closed his eyes and prayed that it would work. The supply of compressed air was not limitless and with the batteries almost exhausted, they would have one chance, and one chance only. The whole crew were willing the boat to move. Several expressed their thoughts verbally, encouraging the sunken beast to stir from her watery grave. Still the air poured into the tanks. They were using everything they had.

Gradually, the stern began to lift, the angle of the deck increased rapidly, and those that had gathered in the engine room now slid uncontrollably back down the deck, trying desperately to hold on to something. Jack Faerber was clinging to a heavy tool box as though his life depended upon it. He could hold it no longer and it plummeted down through the boat taking several cursing crewmen with it. Donald clung to the engine casing for all he was worth. The angle of the boat was now so great that getting to the aft escape hatch was a major mountaineering exercise. The extra weight of the flooded fore-ends had caused the submarine to come up stern first and the bows were still on the seabed. Above the waves several feet of the boat stuck out at 45 degrees in full view.

On the German minesweeper, Ordinary Seaman Freidrich Meier was first to spot *Starfish* surfacing and he immediately sounded the alarm. Within seconds the area was illuminated by powerful searchlights. The fate of *Starfish* was now sealed as the last of the air was blasted into her tanks. The bows started to lift, but with so much weight for'ard she settled bow down in the water with only her conning tower, gun mounting and stern above sea level.

The crew waited anxiously below the escape hatch and Turner proceeded on to the deck casing through the engine room. All thoughts now were on getting out while they had a chance. If *Starfish* went down again that would be the end of them. As soon as Turner emerged into the cold night air the light from the escape hatch was seen by the Germans and they opened fire. Turner wasted no time.

"Abandon ship."

The men reacted quickly. Somebody called out "Married men first" but nobody took any notice. Turner shouted to Dodsworth to open the flood valves. His only priority was to get his men off and ensure that his boat did not fall into enemy hands. Bitterly cold air was now streaming into the boat and mixing with the high levels of carbon dioxide already present. The result was that the boat filled with a fog-like atmosphere, causing even more panic amongst the men as they coughed and spluttered and strained their eyes to see. Donald's turn came and he pulled himself out of the stricken submarine into the freezing night air.

He had a job to hold on to the casing of *Starfish* because of the angle of the stern. She was now starting to list to one side, so much so that water was starting to lap into the open hatch. Donald had never felt so cold before in his life. The icy wind cut right through his flimsy overalls and he could not stop himself from shivering uncontrollably. He dropped down on to his haunches and slid down the submarine's hull into the murky waters below. As soon as he hit the water, breath was forced out of his body. The sea was so cold that in places ice was forming on the surface. His head slipped below the surface as the momentum of his descent carried him downwards.

For a moment he panicked. Unable to breathe, his clothing now weighing about three times its normal weight, he kicked wildly in the water. His head finally broke the surface and icy spray whipped up by driving wind lashed into his face. Survival was now the game and he realised that with no life-saving gear on, he was not going to be able to stay afloat for very long. Already, after no more than a couple of minutes, he could feel the muscles in his arms and legs becoming numb and useless. He was starting to lose the fight to survive.

Around him more men were thrashing about in the water, trying desperately to stay afloat. Harry Shipp and one of the Able Seamen, Irvine, swam past Donald making for the lights that shone brightly in the distance. The German minesweeper M7 had called for assistance from another vessel in the area, M5, and both waited to see what action the submarine would take. The commander feared that *Starfish* would explode either from the damage sustained, or even possibly from her own scuttling charges. He was not prepared to risk his own vessel by going too close, but once he saw figures entering the water and others clinging to the submarine he ordered the cease-fire of his machine guns and lowered dinghies under the command of Leutnant von Haxthausen to pick up survivors. He started to approach the submarine with the intention of arresting the crew still left on board and also to get a line on to her with the hope of towing her back to Wilhelmshaven. To this end he issued an order to Walter Nischann to be ready with a line and marker buoys as soon as they came alongside the stricken submarine.

Shouts and screams filled the air as the men in the water started to drift away from the side of *Starfish.* The surface of the sea was now covered in oil, and that, mixed with spray, was flung into the faces of survivors. Donald was drifting farther and farther away and was slowly losing the strength in both his arms. Above him the tracer bullets that had looked like a firework display suddenly stopped and an eerie silence prevailed. Donald looked back at *Starfish,* which was now completely illuminated by the searchlights, giving her an almost ghostly image against the dark night and heaving sea. In the light he saw Wardle, the torpedo officer, throw something heavy from the bridge that sank as soon as it hit the waves. Donald assumed it must have been the Code Book chest. He wondered how he had managed to get it that far as it weighed a ton.

From alongside Wardle the First Officer, Kyrke, made an almost perfect swallow dive. He tried to make out the other figures still clinging to the casing, Fergie Molloy, Tickler Smith, Ernie Redgate, Stepp, Tindall, Meyer and the tall figure of Bartram. Suddenly out of the gloom came Donald's first view of the enemy. A minesweeper had come alongside *Starfish* and in the heavy swell was trying to get a line across to her. After several attempts she succeeded and moored herself alongside the submarine, which was now settling in the water and threatening to sink. Frenzied activity was going on on board the German vessel and Donald could just make out figures on *Starfish* raising their hands above their heads.

Most of the figures still left on the deck just stepped neatly aboard. For the first time, Donald noticed the state of the submarine. The deck plates were warped and in some places completely missing. The three-inch gun was twisted and warped like a corkscrew. The conning tower looked as though a maniac with a sledgehammer had been let loose again and the mast top was unrecognisable. The Germans appeared to be trying to get a line on the stern of the boat in an attempt to stop her going down, but it seemed a futile exercise. The boat was flooding fast and with each second was settling lower and lower in the water. Unless the Germans released the mooring cables they, too, would be dragged down.

Donald was now shaking uncontrollably from the cold. He summoned every ounce of strength left in his body to try to propel himself towards the relative safety of the German minesweeper. Before he could get anywhere near, another vessel, which looked like a converted trawler, appeared amongst the swimming figures. Donald noticed the swimming figure of Jack Faerber in front of him, closely followed by another of the stokers, Hawkins. Jack got to the trawler first and hauled himself out of the water. Before he could swing his legs over the side, the exhausted shape of Hawkins arrived directly below Jack and made a despairing grab for his legs. The extra weight was too much even for the strong, well-built Faerber and both figures tumbled back into the water. Donald gasped, a combination of tiredness and the sight of the two stokers tumbling back into the water, with Jack issuing a series of curses at Hawkins. Donald gulped in a mouthful of sea water and oil and immediately vomited. He was by now clinging with both hands, his knuckles brilliant white, to the side of the trawler, determined that he was not going to let go.

Before he could do anything else, two pairs of hands plucked him from the water and deposited him on to the deck. He now had his first look at the enemy. Around him lay the prostrate figures of his companions. Many were coughing and chocking or just being sick. Donald focused his attention on the two men standing over him. He looked straight into the barrel of a rifle. Behind it stood a man of about his own age, but there the similarity ended. Donald looked like a drowned rat. His overalls were dripping wet and stained with oil and grime, he had no shoes on his feet, and was shivering uncontrollably. The German, however, was well-dressed for the conditions. A leather jacket kept the wind from cutting through him and he had a pair of waterproof trousers of obvious good quality. Donald thought they were without doubt better equipped than we were.

If the propaganda was correct, Donald was expecting to be smashed with the rifle. Instead the German sailor muttered something he could not understand, lowered his rifle, and tossed Donald a blanket. The other German beckoned the men to their feet. As they stood up they witnessed a sight that none of them would ever forget. The Germans were frantically trying to release their line on to *Starfish,* which was now going through its final death throes. The submarine had keeled over at a sickening angle and the stern was beginning to lift out of the water. Slowly, almost dramatically, the stern pitched into the air and again, almost as if apologising, slid below the waves for the last time.

Waiting for the Gunlayer

By Fred Bunting

I could see Monte Carlo
If it wasn't so dark, and rough,
And pouring with rain.
I could be in my hammock
In the stinking fore ends,
But the gunlayer's late again.

I thought we'd roll over
When we surfaced last night,
Staggering beam on to the sea,
With the diesels pounding
And the Mistral blowing,
Gosport's where I'd rather be.

The new sub-lieutenant's eager for war,
An eager, know-nothing twit,
But when the hunting begins
And we are the fox,
His ardour will cool a bit.

The crew of that U-boat
We missed yesterday
Are ashore, dancing, drinking and fighting,
While I'm out here
Peering into the night
And my lice biting, biting, biting.

Dawn's coming up
And it's "Clear the bridge!"
Ready to take to the deep.
But when the klaxon blares
And the boat plunges down,
The gunlayer will still be asleep!

The Last Voyage of the Pandora

By G. Jenkins

Just before the completion of our refit at the submarine base at Portland, Maine, along with *Truant,* our skipper J. W Linton was relieved by R. L. Alexander, "Tubby" Linton taking over *Turbulent.* We left the U.S.A. but had to put in to Bermuda owing to the loss of lubricating oil. We left Bermuda and crossed the Atlantic to tie up alongside the Maidstone at Gib in March, 1942. *Parthian* was also there but left on March 13-14. We loaded two of our fuel groups with petrol, ammunition and supplies, then left for Malta.

On the third day out something scraped along our starboard saddle tank – we were dived at the time. We arrived at Malta on April 1 and tied up at the jetty. Our skipper had gone ashore to make his report and we discharged our load of petrol. In the meantime, a number of our crew had gone over to the dockyard to stand by and unload the next of our cargo. Speed was essential owing to the heavy air raids. We were going across the harbour on our motors and a number of us decided to have a breather on the casing.

Seven of us went up through the after hatch and there were eight on the bridge, including our engineer, Hickman. We were nearly across the harbour when an air raid started. We managed to tie up port side alongside the dockside.

The raid was now intense and everyone on shore had gone into the shelters. Someone in our bunch shouted that he was going down below (to dodge bomb splinters). As I was the first on the casing I was the last to go down when I noticed that no one was firing any gun from our bridge. By this time I could have almost hit a plane with a potato. I had reached the conning tower casing and the last rungs to the bridge when we received a direct hit. Some soldiers on a gunsight stated that a flame shot up the conning tower like a blow torch and later it was stated that parts of the engine-room were found ashore in the dockyard. I don't remember anything after the explosion until I came to in St Patrick's Hospital at 0300. *Pandora* had been hit almost 12 hours earlier at 1345. I was lucky only to be suffering from shock and blast and injuries to my left hand. I had been in the water but who fished me out and how I got to hospital I don't know. I tried to find out later but failed.

I joined the base at Manoel and joined working parties. One job we got was to get the "tacks" and toilet out of P39, who had broken her back and was on a sand bar. At that time we lost *Upholder* and *Urge.* By a twist of fate quite a few of us took passage on the *Clyde* to Gibraltar. They had emptied one battery space for that purpose. I've often wondered if any of the crew of the *Pandora* who were not on her when she was hit, took passage on the *Olympus* when she hit a mine. I had a chat with my mate Banjo Best, who was S.P.O. of *Olympus* just before they left Malta for Gib. He went down with her.

The control room of Pandora, complete with wooden chest and fittings to give a touch of the "old Navy." Even Nelson would have been at home with the splendid steering and hydroplane wheels.

P.39 and Olympus

by W. G. Wright

After three years and ten months away from home, I finally made it via *Otus, Odin, Rorqual* and *Pandora.* After my experiences in these boats, I asked my fiancee – to whom I had been engaged for six years – whether she wanted to be a young widow or an old maid. She took the chance and we were married in February, 1941 – and still are 43 years later. After too short a leave, I was sent to Barrow-in-Furness as the C.E.R.A. to stand by the building of P.39 at the Vickers Armstrong yard.

The business of "standing by" for a C.E.R.A. is to live in lodgings ashore and to go daily (and often at night) to the boat to learn everything possible about her, particularly the operation of all machinery, air, oil and water systems. A week or two after arriving in Barrow I was sent to Lincoln to see the completion and running trials of the Paxman engines being built for my boat by Ruston Hornsby. When the trials were finished I refused to accept one engine because the crankcase leaked oil. The works manager put pressure on me to accept it, saying "What's a little leak like that?" to which I replied "A jolly lot, especially in the Mediterranean where it would leave a slick of oil after pumping out the bilges." I phoned and wrote a confirming letter to the Naval Engineer Overseer at Barrow, who supported me, and the crankcase had to be made good at some inconvenience to Rustons.

When I got back to Barrow, some more of the E.R.A.s and crew had arrived. I had the arrangement of taking some of my E.R.A.s and engine room staff in parties of three or four through the boat during the dockyard workers' lunch hour. This had the advantage of moving more freely through the empty boat and seeing and explaining pump systems, periscope hoists, air compressors, steering gear and so forth. This practice was somewhat resented by some of my crew because it wasted some of their beer time with their chums from P38, whose C.E.R.A. did not use the same arrangement for training.

Among my stokers were a solicitor's clerk, a pit boy, a cinema attendant and a farmer's boy. These lads had only been to sea for training in old first world war H and L class submarines, so you can see why I was so keen on training them. Sometimes, of course, I could not answer their questions but I soon found the answers. Incidentally, the solicitor's clerk and the farmer's boy became real pals – the clerk was fascinated by the farmer's stories of rabbit-hunting with ferrets and such like.

The First Lieutenant joined the boat when I came back from Rustons and found that I was doing these training sessions when the boat was empty and pipes and valves could easily be seen before the floor plates were put down. He booked one or two lessons to learn the pumping and trimming lines, which would be his job when he went to sea.

At last (all too soon for some of us) our engine trials were completed and the boat handed over to the captain. It was now ours. The next thing was to go up to Arrochar at the top end of Loch Long for torpedo firing trials. These are not so much for testing the torpedo sights as for checking the setting of the Automatic Inboard Venting (AIV) valves. When a torpedo is fired the tube is full of water and torpedo and compressed air is used to force the torpedo out of the tube. As the torpedo is about to leave the tube the AIV valve is suddenly opened and the compressed air pushing out the torpedo is allowed to rush back into the boat. This is to prevent a bubble of air rising to the surface and showing that a torpedo has been fired. The AIV valve is then suddenly shut, but only after it has let some water (about 28 gallons) into a tank directly beneath the torpedo tube. This water compensates for the additional weight of a fully-charged torpedo and so the trim of the submarine remains unchanged. These trials take anything from a couple of days to a week to complete. We took a week to satisfy the trials officers.

The general routine was to load up with torpedoes, go down the Loch and fire them back up the Loch, making adjustments to the AIV after each shot, then of course, back up the Loch for another load of torpedoes to see if the adjustments were effective. The seamen worked hard to get the torpedoes loaded and when that was done the First Lieutenant let them have the afternoon off. They were soon on their way up to the Tarbert Hotel. In peacetime this hotel got large supplies of beer but in wartime there were no visitors except for the sailors, so sailors were allowed to drink at any hour. I did not agree with this and kept my staff working on the little but necessary jobs such as stopping oil leaks from the air compressors and adjusting the refrigerators, etc. until 4 o'clock in the afternoon. Besides that, I also thought that anyone can drink as much as he likes after 4 o'clock. In fact we did lose one man, a Scottish fisherman who fell over the side of a rowing boat that we used as a ferry and drowned.

One afternoon I walked into the engine room, where one of the jobs in hand was tightening down the cylinder head bolts. The solicitor's clerk was in the narrow space between engine and hull and the farmer's boy was on the platform between the engines. The solicitor's clerk was saying "A bloody bastard of a Chief we've got, all the others are up at the Tarbert Hotel by now." A quite viperous hiss from the farmer's boy shut him up and I turned round and walked back into the control room as if I had heard nothing. This action was to serve me in good stead in Gibraltar.

We then had noise trials, in which we were hung between what appeared to be two battleship's buoys in Gare Loch and stopped all machinery. Machines such as ballast pumps were then started up and the noise emitted was registered on listening stations on each side of the loch. Adjustments were made to the pump feet or extra insulation fitted until the noise emission was satisfactory, after which we "steamed" up and down the loch dived on both propellers, then one propeller and at various speeds to determine our most silent speed when dived. Unfortunately we had no most silent speed as both propellers "sang" at any speed, so we had to go into a floating dock – at Dunoon, I think it was – to change our props. We had no dockyard help except for the dock master and the crane driver. We were given one night to do the job and had to be out of the dock by 0830. It snowed and it was cold, but we did it with no time to spare. When the dock was flooded down and we were beginning to slide out I was called up to the conning tower. The dock master was waving a telegram for me, so I shouted at him to read it to me. He shouted back: "A daughter, both doing well." That was December 8, 1941. The captain gave me 48 hours to go to Portsmouth to see them.

We left England on December 16, 1941. P39 was a small boat of 600 tons, 191 feet long, 16 feet in diameter and with a speed of 11.5 knots. All tanks were inside the pressure hull so that any tanks that leaked did so into the boat and in particular any oil that leaked did not leave a slick on the surface. O, P, and R class submarines had riveted external fuel tanks which were notorious for leaks and probably contributed to their terrible slaughter when they came to the Mediterranean. With a perfectly circular hull and with no saddle tanks we did roll in the Bay of Biscay but, of course, we dived during the hours of daylight, which gave us some respite.

There were whispers that the captain of P38 had bet our captain that he would make Gibraltar in the shortest time. P38 had left the day before us because our submarines never sailed in company in those days. As soon as we left the Clyde, the captain rang "Full Speed" on the engine room telegraph. I thought: "If I'm going to be the engineer of this boat, I'm going to be a proper one" so I went along to the wardroom, where the captain had just arrived from the conning tower, and asked him if it was really necessary to order full speed. He said: "Since when has a C.E.R.A. had the right to query the captain's orders?" I replied that I thought the engines might be damaged and said he would not take out a brand new car and run it at full speed, but would run it in for about 500 miles at a moderate speed. He said he wanted full speed, so I said I would get the Engine Room Register for him to sign. He asked me what I meant. I replied: "The King's Rules and Admiralty Instructions say that if a captain gives an order which the engineer officer thinks is detrimental to the engines the captain shall sign the Engine Room Register as to the orders he has given." He was obviously furious but after a long pause ordered "Half speed ahead." I bet he thought he had a sea lawyer for a C.E.R.A.

We were due to arrive in Gibraltar at 1000 hours and I told the stoker P.O. to turn the morning watch to when they had had their breakfast to pump out the bilges, thoroughly clean up our parts of the boat, and in particular the engine room so that it was cleaner than when we had left Vickers. This caused more rumblings about the C.E.R.A. that they were afflicted with. We tied up alongside P38, which in turn was tied up alongside the depot ship *Maidstone,* so we had to cross P38 to get to *Maidstone.* I did not leave P39 for some time as I was expecting the Engineer Commander to come down to inspect my engine room, all the engineering equipment such as steering gear, periscopes and so forth. He would also inspect the engine room register and from it ascertain the amount of fuel oil required to produce one horsepower. After inspection he complimented me on the efficiency and cleanliness of my engine room and on those grounds saw the First Lieutenant to grant my engineroom staff a "make and mend," i.e. the afternoon off.

Just after this the solicitor's clerk came to me and said "Have you been over to P38?" When I said I had not he said that I ought to. "She's like a public lavatory with cylinder heads everywhere, and they are grinding in the cylinder head seats and have to work day and night until the job's finished. None of them have been ashore yet." I said: "Do you remember calling me all the bastards under the sun when you were tightening up the cylinder head bolts in Loch Long? No doubt you were also cursing me for turning you to this morning to clean the boat up." He did not know where to put his face. I said: "Wait a minute, don't run away. P38's troubles are due to her crew not taking care of her and if some of these troubles had occurred when she was in a tight corner she might not be here to tell the tale. Whilst I am C.E.R.A. on this boat I am going to see that she is in an efficient state as is within my power to maintain her. I don't care whether you drown or not but I'm not going to let you drown me if I can possibly help it.

"We have been complimented by the Engineer Commander from the *Maidstone* on the efficiency and cleanliness of this boat and I have seen the First Lieutenant to give leave from 1200 hours to all of my departments who can be spared. So off you go to see the Spanish dancing girls."

From the *Maidstone* we carried out two or three patrols up the Spanish coast and around the French Riviera. We did not attack any ships for real but we carried out dummy attacks, taking note of the ship's name and the flag under which she was sailing, mostly Vichy French. We continually carried out practice crash dives and we had got our time down to 60 seconds by the time we left the *Maidstone.* We then said goodbye to Gibraltar and set sail for Malta, again following P38. While on passage we were generally given a bombing restriction area, that is an area where friendly aircraft were not to bomb submarines, and of course it changed from day to day. Halfway between Gib and Malta the captain sent for me and said: "Chief, I want full speed tonight as soon as we surface. The bombing restriction areas allocated to us from Gibraltar and those allocated from Malta have a gap between them. With a bit of luck we can surface early, dive late and we ought to be somewhere near the Malta area. Bring your register along and I'll sign it."

"There's no need for that, sir" I said. "The engines have been well run in now." I stayed in the engine room all night, from the moment we surfaced at about dusk until dawn had broken when we dived. We just made it into our bombing restricted area and I was thanked by the captain. From then on, we got on.

We arrived in Malta, where special arrangements had been made for entering harbour. One could only enter in daylight and on the surface. If a large red air raid warning flag was flying from the top of the Citadel, one had to remain dived. We now belonged to the 10th Flotilla, commanded by Captain "Shrimp" Simpson. I never knew of anyone dodging a patrol – these were usually kept down to 12 days or whenever all torpedoes were expended. On one occasion I saw a gun layer struggling with his coxswain, he was fighting drunk. The coxswain was shouted at by Captain Simpson to get a heaving line, tie it round the drunk and throw him in the creek. He was then hauled out and continued to refuse to return to his boat, cursing everyone and telling them what he thought about their parents, so he was thrown in again. After three or four times of this treatment he gave in and went back to his boat, which almost immediately cast off. Incidentally, nothing more was done about the matter.

We carried out a couple of short patrols from Malta. One was uneventful, and on the other we came across, or rather they came across us, a well-escorted convoy which dropped 60 depth charges on us in as many minutes. As long as it does no harm, this is the stuff to make an efficient crew. Not that I wasn't frightened. When we came back to harbour the red flag was not flying so we surfaced and identified ourselves. Down came a Messerschmitt, which put a line of bullets along our hull. He did no damage to the hull but he hit the ventilation pipe.

In March, 1941, the boat was lying at the end of one of the catwalks in the creek when there was an air raid. I was in the mess ashore when I heard that P39 had been hit. I rushed over the catwalk to find that it had been a near miss, not a direct hit, but it had caused considerable damage throughout the boat including severe damage to the batteries, which had to be removed. From this time we began to suffer from more and more serious air raids. On March 26 we came out of the shelters to find our boat in a very sorry state, almost broken in half. This was the end of P39.

Conditions in Malta were becoming untenable and I believe it was decided to evacuate the 10th Flotilla. Anyhow the complete crew of P39 was to return to the U.K. on board *Olympus* and were to take over the first completed U class from Vickers at Barrow. The crew of P36 were to follow and take the next one.

We left harbour in the dark at 4 o'clock in the morning. At 5 o'clock there was a big bang and I, being "bomb happy" from the months in Malta, rushed into the control room to be ready to dive the boat. Geordie Talbot, the outside E.R.A. whose job it was, arrived as soon as I did so I went back to the engine room. The port engine telegraph went to "Stop" and Sammy stopped it and said "Shall I shut it down for diving?" I said that I would. The other engine was still going and it felt to me that we were turning in a tight circle. Then the starboard telegraph went to "Stop" so I stopped it and ordered the stokers to shut it down for diving. Then I nipped into the control room to see what was happening because we had seen some stokers coming from aft. One of them said "It's abandon ship" but we heard nothing.

When I got into the control room it was ankle deep in water and there were some flashes and the lights went out and quickly on again with the roll of the boat. Back I rushed into the engine room and shouted "Abandon ship." In the control room I saw the engineering officer of *Olympus* standing at the bottom of the conning tower ladder controlling the flow of about 12 to 15 people going up the ladder. I thought "This is going to take a little time" and at the same time as the boat rolled, the water was touching the switches for longer and longer periods. Looking along the empty gangway towards the fore ends I saw that the boat's galley had been displaced into the gangway and that was where the water was rushing in. I also thought that I saw the yellow fumes of chlorine.

Olympus pictured at Portsmouth in 1930. She sank in just nine minutes in 1941 after hitting a mine in the swept channel leading out from Malta.

Time was getting short and I took the risk and went forward to the gun tower ladder. At the bottom of this ladder was Lieut. Bulmer of P39, who appeared to have been controlling here but now had no queue. As soon as he saw me he cheerfully said "Come on chief, up you go." Some others from the control room must have followed me because he was not immediately behind me. As I came up the blackouts were becoming longer due to the slower rolls caused by the amount of free surface water.

As I came out of the gun tower hatch I saw that about 90 men were out of the boat, most of them standing on the forecasing. Looking up to the conning tower I saw my captain trying to signal towards Malta with a hand torch. Apparently the distress flares fitted on the periscopes had failed to ignite – this was later confirmed by one of the survivors who had been up on the conning tower. Neither could the Aldis lamp be brought into use. Malta could be seen as a shadow on the horizon and a plane was flying above it with a very small yellow light.

On the gun tower platform they were trying to fire the four-inch gun, but they could not close the breech. We tried to remove the shell from the breech but it separated and still left the projectile jammed. I had seen cordite burnt when I was an apprentice so I shouted up to the bridge. "Can we tip the cordite out of the cartridge and burn it?" I knew this would mean clearing a large area of the boat and laying a fuse but we were desperate. Captain Dymott of *Olympus* shouted back "Do what you like." Then we saw that the bows of the boat were going under water. We took off our shoes and put them in pairs around the gun stand. As the water came up to the foot of the gun tower I jumped down and took off, swimming away from the sinking boat. When I got about 20 yards away, I turned round to see her slide gently down on her last dive. Even with a lot of people around me I felt lonely.

There was a bit of shouting at first, mainly people seeking their friends, and a few were helping non-swimmers. I had never swum a mile before or anything like it so I kept clear of any involvement because it seemed to me that it would take some time for help to come out to us. The cries for help and friends soon died down and we set off more or less in a group, heading for Malta, from which direction we expected help to come. One or two people had Davis escape apparatus, but that hindered swimming, and as far as I know no survivors had any form of life-saving gear. We saw a floating mine with what appeared to be a whip aerial with a wire hanging from it and a leading stoker named Hiscock started to swim towards it but the others shouted to him not to blow us up. He heeded our pleas and he survived.

Daylight soon came and Malta became quite clear to see but Oh! what a long way away. It now became a very silent swim and calling out to see how friends were getting on virtually ceased. People were drowning silently, probably from exhaustion, but at least one announced it. "I'm through" he said and put his arms up in the air and went down. I had discarded all of my clothing except for my short pants and navy belt. The belt I had kept because I found a small piece of floating wood that I tucked under it to give me more buoyancy, but it chafed my skin after a while so I threw it away. I still hoped that something more buoyant would turn up.

At 7 o'clock we watched the breakfast time raid on Malta. I suddenly thought that if on the way back the fighter cover saw us they would swoop down and shoot us up. I braced myself to dive under the water if a fighter pointed its nose towards me. How long I would be able to hold my breath I didn't know but I thought it would put a foot or two of water between me and the bullet. In any event they ignored us then and in a couple of other raids we witnessed. "What if they saw us?" I thought, and had the morbid thought of my daughter as she grew up asking my wife "Why haven't I got a daddy like other little girls?" This thought gave me the incentive to keep on going. I started a routine, when I felt really weary, of turning over on my back and floating while I drew in twelve very deep breaths and then turning back and plodding. Our group of swimmers had now become strung out and fewer. Later, when we finally came ashore, it was rumoured that a soldier lookout had, at 8 o'clock in the morning, reported that there were 25 swimmers heading for Malta.

At 10 o'clock in the morning I could see the coast clearly and an ambulance was up on the bank. Two soldiers were watching me intently from the beach. I was very cold and felt as if my whole body were down to the temperature of the sea, which incidentally was 51 degrees Farenheit when I had put the temperature into the ER Register, a long time ago at 4 o'clock. The soldiers were still watching me but making no move of any sort. When I was about ten yards from the beach I called out "Help me" and confidently put my feet down. It was deeper than I thought and I went right under. I came up spewing water and inwardly cursing the soldiers and myself for nearly drowning at this stage in the affair. I then swam breast stroke until my elbows and knees grounded on the beach. The soldiers came into the ankle deep water and put an arm under each of my arms as I stood up.

I knew then that I was safe, and promptly collapsed unconscious.

I came to in the ambulance and one of the soldiers had presumably removed my pants and belt and was rubbing me down. He asked me if I was cold. I looked down at myself and thought "You fool, I'm ruined" then I faded out again. Geordy Talbot, the outside E.R.A. for *Olympus* had stood up and fallen down dead. Later I found out the place where I had come ashore was called Point St Leonardo. No one else appeared to be in the ambulance with me except, of course, the soldiers, and I was taken to an emergency hospital – probably a large confiscated house in the country.

When I came to again I found that there were seven of us in hospital beds in a large room. There were three from *Olympus* and four from P39. We were given a large mug of hot tea and a sandwich. The tea was most welcome and we asked for another mug, which was grudgingly given to us. About this time a soldier came along and laid my pants, navy belt and six pound notes on a chair beside my bed. with one accord the others all called out "That was all you swam ashore for." I was the only property owner among us. At about this time we learned that Gordon Selby, the coxswain, and Sid Seymour, the P.O. L.T.O. of P.39, had been taken to Lazaretto. They were strong swimmers and apparently had landed before us. So up to then there were nine of us who had survived, six from P.39 and three from *Olympus.*

Ginger Hiscock, a leading stoker from P39, kept intoning to me in a solemn voice "As ye sow so shall ye reap." I asked him what he was on about and he replied "You were on *Rorqual,* weren't you?" It hit me like a brick. *Rorqual* was a large minelaying submarine carrying 50 mines and I had indeed been in her laying mines off the North African coast.

By early morning we were ravenous and wanted our breakfast. We were given the usual large mug of tea and a very meagre meal – I cannot remember exactly what it was now, but we thought it was not enough. We wanted more but the soldiers said it was our ration and they had no more. We started moaning for more, but they were probably right about the rations.

In Lazaretto the captain of *Unique,* Lieut. Collett, was of the "landed gentry" type and started a farmyard with a couple of piglets. They were fed on potato peelings and left-overs. It became quite a flourishing little farm to augment our rations. When a bomb fell in the farmyard most of the meat was salvaged – but I digress too much. We griped so much about the Army that the sergeant said he would bring the Major to us. One of the survivors had lost his nerve and said that he was not going to sea again and certainly not on submarines. Actually when we got home he requested to leave submarines, which he did and went to a cruiser (the *Fiji,* I believe it was) and was lost off Crete. We were all sitting on this poor fellow's bed when the sergeant came in with the Major, a doctor, and shouted "Attention in the beds."

We then got into our respective beds and the doctor addressed us. He said that he wanted to keep us for a few days until we were in better health but that if we did not behave ourselves he would send us back to Lazaretto, where they were being bombed four or five times a day. With one accord we said that that was where we wanted to go. He seemed surprised and said "So far we have not had a single bomb here." We said "We want to go back to Lazaretto." He said that he would send us there after he had inspected us to make sure that we were fit to travel. After he had inspected us the ambulance driver came in and was given a receipt which he had to bring back, signed by an officer, confirming that he had delivered seven bodies. The doctor then said "Take them away" and we immediately said "What, like this?" I was a bit smug with my short pants, blue navy belt and six pounds in it. I was sartorially perfect and they were all "starkers." The sergeant and the doctor then got together and decided that we could have one blanket each, which had to be returned, so the receipt was amended. Off we went with the Major clearly thinking "What an unruly and ungrateful mob."

When we got to the little bridge connecting Manoel Island to the main island the ambulance could not get across it. The bridge was not broken but piled high with rocks and debris from near misses, so we had to get out and walk with the ambulance driver following us, intent upon retrieving the blankets. From the bridge to Lazaretto must have been about threequarters of a mile. With our stiff joints, bare feet and the rough terrain, together with the blankets wrapped around our shoulders, we looked like a string of Red Indian squaws.

When we got to Lazaretto we made for the sick bay where we knew we would find our energetic Surgeon Commander. He was soon giving us medical examinations while the ambulance driver kept advancing on him waving the palm of his hand in a real military salute saying "Please, sir." The surgeon would say "Can't you see I'm busy? Get the hell out of it." When it was my turn to be examined the ambulance driver approached again and the surgeon was getting really angry when I piped up and said "It's not really his fault, sir, he has been ordered to take back these blankets and he is trying to get you to give them back and to sign the receipt for us." The surgeon then promptly settled with the driver and said "Have you been walking barefooted? Where from?" and I told him. He said "Is this all the clothing you have?" He then sent for the C.P.O. in charge of the dead men's clothing store, finished our examinations, and told the C.P.O. to take us up to the store and fix us up. Incidentally, the surgeon said to me "How old are you?" I said 32, and he asked me if I had done much swimming, I replied that I had never swum more than a mile before. He said that it was not bad for someone of my age. I asked how far it was and he said about seven miles.

We were to return to the U.K. in a fast minelayer, *H.M.S. Welshman.* We left Grand Harbour and headed for Gibraltar at 39 knots, the ship disguised as a French Simoon Class destroyer. We had a couple of unwelcome visits from German aircraft on the way. I eventually reached U.K. and after a spell of leave "stood by" P314, later to be named *Tactician.* I served two years in her, first in the Mediterranean and then, when Italy surrendered in the Far East, mainly in the Malacca Straits. When we obtained the U1407 I became her C.E.R.A. She was propelled under water by hydrogen peroxide engines.

The Seadog

by Scratcher

We had a little doggy
Who was white as Pusser's Grey
Often did he wander
Through our boat every day.

He'd never seen a baa-lamb
No cow nor trees or grass
He'd never even seen his dad
And so it came to pass.

It was a rusty "T" boat
With doggy watches, too,
And into Derry did we steam
With pounds to spend a few.

A bread van used to call on us
The buns we did adore.
By bribing driver with a tot,
He got his run ashore.

Eventually in Malta,
Where the land is so bare,
A wiser dog called Snowy
Who doesn't seem to care.

As for cows, trees and grass
Little does he say
But the run when he met a bitch
Hooray, hooray, hooray.

Now all the dogs in Malta
Talk of Snowy's run ashore
And of a magic bread van
And of a Paradise amour.

But somewhere in Ireland
Amid the fields so green
Lives a little Snow-pup
Who talks of father unseen.

Also in that Emerald Isle
As a result of that run
Waits a farmer and his bitch
And a loaded shot gun.

Upholder

Author's name unknown

Went to Barrow-in-Furness to stand by submarine *Upholder* on about September 22, 1940. She was in the final stages of her building at this time. Commissioned on October 16 and went to Scotland for trials.

Did our trials in Loch Long and visited a few other places around there, our depot ship during this time being *H.M.S. Forth,* which was moored off Dunoon. Left Scotland for Portsmouth and there had foreign service leave.

Sailed from U.K. and arrived in Gibraltar just before the New Year, spending Christmas at sea. In Gibraltar for a while, then we sailed for Malta, arriving about three weeks later.

Our first sinking, just off Tripoli, Tuesday, January 28, 1941 at 1427. We fired two fish from Nos 1 and 2 tubes at a convoy and scored one hit on a cargo ship of about 5,000 tons. She took a long while to go down but eventually went bows first.

Thursday, January 30, off Tripoli, time 1619, we fired two more fish, from tubes three and four, at an escorted convoy. One hit on an 8,000-ton supply ship. We received 32 depth charges pretty close but managed to get away under cover of darkness.

As we came off patrol we had some torpedoes fired at us by an enemy submarine but we dived out of the way.

About April 10 we fired four fish in two salvoes at a convoy. These were our last torpedoes and it was starting to get dark so we surfaced and warned Base of the position of the convoy but it must have altered course because our aircraft couldn't find it.

We saw a convoy on the following night just as it was getting dark but having no torpedoes left we surfaced and fired star shells over the convoy to give away their position to any of our aircraft that may have been about. We expected a few depth charges in exchange but were pleasantly disappointed. A flotilla of destroyers later wiped out that convoy.

On Friday April 25, 1941, off Tripoli at 1531 we fired at a convoy getting one hit, a cargo ship of about 7,900 tons.

Saturday, April 26, west of Tripoli, at 2030 we went alongside the *Arta,* an Italian supply ship wiped up by destroyers. We sent a boarding party aboard but all they found was a good few German soldiers and a good stink coming from them. On blowing the safe they set fire to the ship but did manage to get her papers all right. They had to come off quickly as the ship began to blaze up but they did bring with them a few tommy guns, a few tin hats, a Nazi ensign and a lot of other junk. The ship was last seen blazing on the horizon.

Sunday, April 27, we tried to get alongside a destroyer wiped out in the same convoy, but ran aground before we could do so and had to put the blower on all tanks to get her off again.

We came off that patrol with a guard of honour on the far casing wearing German tin hats, carrying German tommy guns and flying the German ensign.

Thursday, May 1, at 1146 we fired at a convoy getting three hits on three separate targets – a destroyer, a 4,000-ton supply ship and a 10,000-ton supply ship. The first two sank and the third came to a standstill. Another destroyer crept up to the 10,000-tonner in the hope of towing her off so at 1901 we slammed two more fish into the supply ship, which was last seen upside down on the surface before she sank. We could not stop to see her sink as we were too busy dodging depth charges.

Saturday, May 24, 1941. As it was getting dark we sighted a liner with an escort of three cruisers and an uncountable number of destroyers at about 2025.

2030 Diving Stations.

2045 Fired 2 fish, 1 and 4 tubes.

2046 Flood Q, 150 feet.

As we dived we heard both torpedoes explode on target. Depth charges started dropping after the torpedoes exploded. Thirty-three were dropped on us, very close. Destroyers passed right overhead twice. I was pretty shaky, could not stop legs from shaking, but did not let anybody notice it.

2126 Depth charges stopped.

2140 Came up to 70 feet.

2145 Watch diving.

2238 Diving stations.

2247 Surface, terrible smell of oil fuel on surface when I went up as lookout. We had scored two hits on a liner of about 18,000 tons carrying about 4,000 troops.

Thursday, July 3, we sighted a small convoy and at 1142 we fired 2 and 4 tubes at a timber ship of some 6,000 tons. We got one hit on the target and had 19 charges dropped but not too close.

Thursday, July 24. 1345, sighted an Italian destroyer and a 6,000-ton merchant ship.

1412 Stand by.

1416 Fire a salvo of three from tubes 1, 2 and 3.

One hit on the merchantman. At 1530 she was seen to be down by the stern. We got 18 depth charges, which they continued to drop until pretty late when we were well away from the spot.

Monday, July 28, we sighted a convoy at 1951 firing a salvo of four and getting two hits on a cruiser of 7,280 tons. We received 42 charges very near. Indeed, once when we were expecting to hear the next one explode we heard one of the destroyers pass right overhead and, boy, we had our hearts in our mouths. The cruiser was of the D'Aosta class. We had one torpedo left and later went back and fired on the convoy but missed.

We came back through the minefield on Wednesday, July 30.

August 5, sent to prison for 30 days for losing my temper with a colonel in the Army and insulting a petty officer.

September 1, my day of freedom, got drafted to spare crew.

October 17, drafted to SM *Ursula.*

October 18, 1941, on our way to southern Italy, at 0616 we sighted a convoy of four cargo ships with a three-ship destroyer escort. At 0801 we fired 1, 2, 3 and 4 tubes and got hits on two ships of about 6,000 and 7,000 tons. In return we received five depth charges.

October 23, at 1345 we surfaced and fired 87 rounds at a railway bridge. We did considerable damage to the bridge, but had to break off and dive out of the way owing to the breech jamming. Their coastal defence opened up at us but only with a machine gun that simply made a few dents in the control tower.

Sunday, November 30, we set out for home. Will be glad to see the folks at home.

Diving Stations

by Mick Jones

The silence of the boat is rent
By the klaxon's raucous, strident note.
The outside Tiffy opens vents
To flood the tanks and dive the boat.

Foreplanes put to "hard-a-dive,"
Telegraphs both to "half ahead."
L.T.O.s at breakers strive
Take her down, the klaxon said.

"Jimmy" jumps from aft to for'ard,
Does his best to catch the trim.
Skipper mutters something horrid,
Implies that Jimmy's bloody dim.

Trim is caught and hearts stop pounding,
All is once again serene.
Such is life at klaxon's sounding
On board a British submarine.

Trusty

by S. G. Hillyard

We received our sailing orders for the evening of February 7, 1942, and so we left Kepple Harbour and Singapore. We took no passengers and our destination was the port of Sumatra on Java. About six miles out of Singapore we looked back and saw great pillars of fire on Singapore Island. Presumably our Royal Engineers had demolished the oil storage tanks, or had the Japanese over-run the colony? As we came to know later, the surrender was signed without a shot being fired.

We settled into our usual patrol routine, two hours on and four hours off watch, diving during the day, surfacing at dusk and diving again at dawn. Conditions in *Trusty* were not too good. Humidity was such that we were continually perspiring whilst dived, so that when we lay down on bunks or hammocks, we lay in a pool of sweat. This gave us prickly-heat – the body develops spots which are extremely itchy and make life very uncomfortable. As these spots must not be rubbed and as we were only allowed to use salt water for a sluice down, we just let the sweat come off dry at night when we surfaced. We must have hummed to high heaven.

Passing Sumatra on our starboard, we cruised out with Borneo to port. On February 9 we had surfaced as usual at dusk. It was a beautiful evening with millpond sea, full moon and the stars so clear in all their glory. We ate our evening meal, cleared up and settled down for the night. My watch was from 2200 to midnight, which is called the second part of the first watch, and my patrol duties were lookout – in those days two ratings and the Officer of the Watch up on the upper tower.

We had extremely powerful binoculars which we used for the whole watch. Before lookouts went up top they had to spend ten minutes in the dark so that they could see properly as soon as they arrived on watch. After a while imagination begins to try to take over and clouds on the horizon tend to look like ships, so you shift the glasses from that spot and go back to it a minute later – and there it is, a curiously-shaped cloud. I enjoyed those lookout watches – fresh air, romantic moonlight, the white spume passing by from the bows pushing through the sea and the vibrations of the diesel engines below.

At midnight the reliefs took over. We stayed there until they were accustomed to the dark, a little banter, and down we went. Everybody not on watch had turned in. It seemed strange, on reflection, how we managed to sleep as the lights were permanently on, but we were so young that a clothes line as a bed would have been no problem.

I moved for'ard to the fore-ends, where the spare torpdoes were stowed, and settled down until 0400, but it was not to be because just before 0100, I was shaken awake.

"Gun Action."

What was it? A man of war, big or little? Merchant ship? Small junk? How far away? Thousands of thoughts flashed through my mind as I made my way to the gun hatch (we never undressed on patrol so no time was lost dressing).

My gun action duty was that of shell loader and, because I had to push a 4.5in. shell into the breech of the gun, I had acquired a right-hand wicket keeper's glove to protect my knuckles. Soon we were assembled at the gun, the gunlayer, a gun trainer for elevation or lateral movement and me. Then there were the ammunition carriers, who started in the magazine locker. Our cook was stationed here, with seamen stationed at intervals to pass the shells to me.

Our target was a merchantman of 8,000 or 10,000 tons which was about a mile away. I pushed home a shell, closed the breech and waited. They must have had slack lookouts because there was no sign of activity on the darkened ship. Lieut.-Commander Bill King was at the for'ard part of the conning tower while the navigating officer, who was also the gunner officer, stood under it on the upper deck casing just to the rear of the gun. The orders came.

"Bear on the radio mast, up elevation."

Would the gun-layer never squeeze the trigger? The waiting was intolerable.

"Fire," and again a direct hit. "Bear on the superstructure." Direct hits. We were getting in close.

"Bear on the waterline." We were now in what is termed "battle tension." I was busy ramming shells home when she started to sink, bows down.

An orange flash came from the stern deck of the merchantman – they were firing at us. The first went over us, the second hit the underside of the gun but we were all alive.

"Bear on the gun."

The second shell was enough to silence it, or did the machine guns finish them?

"Cease fire," from the navigating officer. "Close up the gun and clear decks."

I was the last to go down the perpendicular gun tower ladder. A shout from below. "Who's bleeding?" I looked down and the upturned faces had blood on them. Good god, how did an accident happen down there? But it was blood from my right hand. Due to the extreme tension I had felt no pain until I descended to the lower deck. I looked at my gloved hand – what a mess. It was as if I was looking at another person's hand, just a bloody mess.

By now the pain was evident. The coxswain was our doctor and his knowledge of medicine and surgery were limited to aspirins and No. 9s. Bill King, the skipper, turned the Wardroom into a makeshift surgery and never have so many hands attended to one hand. Soon the glove was off the hand and the wounds cleaned but the fingerss were now like a bunch of bananas.

What do we do now? quoth the skipper. Ah, yes! A book on medical know-how was obtained from his cabin and we watched him flipping through pages.

"Hmm, we've got to beware of gangrene."

My heart sank as I had vision of the cook cutting off my hand and dipping the stump into one of his concoctions to cauterise it.

Somebody suggested morphine and the coxswain rummaged among the medical equipment. Back he came with two phials of morphine, a vicious-looking syringe and a descriptive leaflet. By now I was hypnotised by the look on the coxswain's face. He was a top surgeon, or so his imagination told him. Reading from the leaflet, he drew the morphine from ther phial, and, still reading, pointed the syringe up in the air and pushed the plunger. We all got sprayed with a phial full of morphine. The second attempt was successful, aided by Jimmy the One, who gently restrained the coxswain from giving a repeat spray of the wardroom. So where do we stick him? Much consideration and reading of the book – it was in the arm! I think the vein was missed but the morphine was injected.

I think I awoke 24 hours later (according to the doctor at Ceylon I should have been buried at sea, so lethal a dose was administered). The skipper messed me in the wardroom and I had the novel experience of having officers cutting and dicing my meals so that I could eat them with my left hand.

The remainder of the patrol was uneventful and we arrived at Surabaya ten days later. The situation was chaotic. Singapore had fallen, the Japanese air force was bombing the isles of Java and Sumatra and evacuation was in progress. We took on what stores we could scrounge and I was sent to the Dutch Army M.O., who, after inspecting my hand said: "Sorry, I've not got time to operate as I'm leaving today." However, he dressed my hand and sent me off (by now, new skin had formed over the pieces of shrapnel). We were due to depart the following day so the rest of the day was my own. The Javanese people were charming and very clean, as were their Dutch overlords.

I strolled around and entered a riding stable with about 15 well-cared for hunters. The owners were nowhere to be seen but a stable groom, a small Javanese, all smiles, came to me. We talked in the usual fashion of two people ignorant of each other's language, with our hand and facial expressions and, eventually he saddled up a fine-looking beast, hoisted me up and there I was, my right arm in a sling and a bit wary but the horrse responded to heels and knee pressure so, holding the reins in my left hand, I moved out into the road.

It was very nice, just what the doctor ordered, and we had trotted and walked for about half an hour when events happened over which I had no control. I heard the sound of heavy lorries behind me and looking back, saw a long line of American open lorries crammed with G.I.s. Well! The sight of a British sailor on horseback with an arm in a sling was just too much for them. I heard the whoops and yells as the convoy overtook me – "Ride him, cowboy!" and other endearing epithets! What with the noise of shouting and banging of rifle butts, it was too much for my mount. He took the bit between his teeth and was away like the wind. This excited the G.I.s into greater uproar, which made the horse into the fastest thing in the world, or so it seemed to me.

Fortunately there was a fork in the road ahead and, thankfully the convoy went right and we went left. I was by now holding on for dear life, the reins were over my head and my left arm was locked around the neck of the horse. Whether I was strangling him or not I don't know but eventually he slowed down, steaming and sweating. I felt like a limp rag as we turned round and rode back to the stables, where my Javanese groom was smilingly waiting to help me off. I think the relief was so great that I just slid off and nearly crushed the groom into the ground.

Trusty left Java next day and the island soon fell to the Japanese. Our destination was Colombo, in Ceylon – "The Pearl." Our patrol was for 21 days and I was a little despondent as it would be nearly five weeks before I could get proper treatment but there was nothing to be done but bear it. The patrol was uneventful and we steamed into Colombo to take up our berth alongside the *Lucia,* an old depot ship with concrete decks and a coal burner to boot.

I was soon off to Colombo hospital, a white good-looking building run by nuns and Singhalese doctors. The ward to which I was allotted was full of survivors from *Repulse* and *Prince of Wales.* Most of them had arms and legs amputated but were very cheerful at the prospect of being shipped home. My surgeon informed me that he would try to save my hand and would operate at intervals. He performed two operations, removing the shell fragments, but then R.N. doctors took over the hospital, together with the Royal Alexandra Nursing Corps. Overnight the atmosphere of the hospital changed from an easy-going routine to R.N. discipline, with sheets tucked in by numbers, thermometers in the mouth at the angle of 45 degrees and not forgetting doctor's rounds in the morning with retinue.

During the rounds the Surgeon Commander studied my papers, muttered to the sick bay tiffy and passed on. I learnt from the Chief Tiffy that no more treatment was to be done to my hand. This news left me very depressed, as there was no movement at all in the fingers and they were getting very thin, a wasting process. I felt pretty hopeless – who could help me? My next door neighbour in bed was an Irishman named Paddy Jones, of all the names for an Irsihman. He had not only kissed the Blarney Stone but had swallowed it as well. Being a Catholic he talked me into going to the service in the nuns' chapel each evening.

The singing by the nuns was beautiful and, on the same evening as I had been told about the non-treatment of my hand, I saw the Singhalese surgeon who had operated on my hand. He asked about it and received my news with surprise. The next morning I learnt that the Singhalese surgeon had interceded on my behalf with the R.N. surgeon and he had agreed to carry on operating on my hand. What a relief – and under such strange circumstances. After a month of operations, the surgeon informed me that the remaining fragments were too small to operate on and I was to be sent to Dyatelawa rest camp up in the hills for convalescence. My hand still had no movement as much as I tried to move the fingers.

So I went by train up country. The seats were hard but the scenery as the two-engined train climbed up to the camp was breath-taking and the vast tea plantations were numerous. The rest camp was cosmopolitan and every Allied force had representatives there. The routine was free and easy, the food was not too bad, camp concerts were frequent and hilarious, and for a diversion I used to walk through the jungle to a village called Bandarawala, which boasted a small hotel for the local tea planters, where an excellent dinner was provided if one so desired. I came to know many of the planters and their wives. The climate up there was that of an English summer at its best and I enjoyed every minute of my stay at the camp, but after three weeks I returned to the humid atmosphere of Colombo.

I reported to the surgeon, who asked: "Can you move the fingers yet?" Although I had tried at the camp, my fingers refused to move. What had happened was that part of the brain that gave signals to my hand had shut itself off. I was sent to a psychiatrist on board the R.N. hospital ship. This was a new departure for the medical staff of the R.N. Our first consultation was stilted and I think we were both pleased when he called it a day. We had many more sessions but the fingers were still unmoved and in the end he gave me up as one of his failures.

While I was on the hospital ship for the last consultation I came into conversation with a P.O. Sick Bay Steward. We discussed my hand and agreed to meet ashore again that evening. We met for a meal and over a few drinks afterwards he suggested that if the tendons and sinews in my right arm could be pulled in some way, the fingers might move. Of course, there was the answer: electrodes on my arm over the tendon would cause a shock to make my fingers move. But, how to get the equipment in Colombo? However, by sacrificing my precious tot of rum per day and borrowing many more, I managed to acquire assorted batteries, some wire, spoons for electrodes and a sliding resistance. This I connected together in the sick bay. We were very excited and, with the sliding resistance all in, he applied the spoon to my inner forearm. A tingle. Adjusting the resistance, he tried again. Ah! The most injured finger moved, and then the others. It was painful and I was sweating profusely. The surgeon commander was informed and came to watch the next performance, bringing along many observers. With the fingers moving freely, all were impressed with our Heath Robinson contraption.

After a few more electric shocks, I coould move the fingers on my own and was very pleased. Soon I was discharged as fit, back to *Trusty* and out on to patrol which proved uneventful. When we got back to Colombo, *Truant* had joined us (I had served in her in the Med) and she was ordered on a "Show the flag" tour round the coast of Africa. To my delight I was drafted to *Truant.* I had been away from the U.K. two-and-a-half years and as we moved off from Colombo harbour, I felt very grateful that events had turned out well.

Tally Ho!!

Dedicated to Commander L.W.A. Bennington, D.S.O., D.S.C., R.N., and his officers and crew on their return from the Far East.

A hunting we did go,
A hunting we did go,
A hunting we did go,
On our good ship "Tally Ho," my boys,
Our good ship "Tally Ho."

One morn we spied a Jap,
A cruiser you must know,
Our skipper just went nap,
So we laid the blighter low, my boys,
We laid the blighter low.

A Jap sub came into view,
Our skipper cried "Yo Ho,"
This is no place for two,
So we laid the blighter low, my boys,
We laid the blighter low.

A "chaser" then raced past,
Our skipper gave a frown,
I'll make this chase his last,
So we put the blighter down, my boys,
We put the blighter down.

An escort ship we got,
"Suppy ships" near a score,
We sank the blinking lot
Then looked around for more, my boys,
Then looked around for more.

And now back home in port,
A spending all our dough,
When we are running short,
We'll go back to the old Tally Ho, my boys,
Back to the old Tally Ho.

A-hunting they would go – the crew of Tally Ho!

Unshaken

by Leading Seaman "Sharkey" Ward

An account of the capture and escorting to Malta of the Italian submarine *Menotti*

Unshaken was on patrol off Brindisi on the night Italy ceased hostilities. We surfaced and received the signal that as from 0800 we had to treat them as a surrendered nation. We dived and closed in towards Brindisi. The Captain, J. Whitton, sighted a submarine on the surface and intended to persuade it to surrender to us and to follow us to Malta, or sink it to prevent it being taken over by the Germans, whom we believed were still in control of the Brindisi base. (At this stage I must add that on this patrol we carried a spare C.O. to give him experience. His name was Swanston.)

We went to diving stations – mine was in the fore-ends on the tubes – and I was called into the control room feeling slightly confused as others knew more at the time than I did. I was dressed in khaki shorts and slippers, with my identity disc round my neck and that's all. Upon entering the control room the gun layer, Bill Peck, proceeded to place a lanyard with a pistol attached around my neck and a paper packet in my hand, which I put into my pocket. The captain lowered the periscope, turned his attention to me and proceeded to give me my orders. He told me he had a submarine dead ahead with a lot of ratings on the casing. He indicated that when he gave the order to surface I was to get out of the top lid, over the bridge and on to the casing, by which time the bows of *Unshaken* would be level with the casing of the surfaced submarine. He wanted me to get aboard it and keep the crew off their gun.

I entered the conning tower, took the top lid clips off and waited for ten feet. The captain was right behind me. I was most surprised to find the manoeuvre was executed exactly as the skipper had said it would be. I was out, over and down in a flash and stepped on to their casing. I waved the gun at the startled crew as they rushed forward, and they retreated to the conning tower. The two captains then proceeded to try to converse.

"Have you had the signal?" Our captain made himself understood with the aid of sign language.

"Yes," replied the Italian captain, but he was still doubtful and wanted to go into Brindisi to check. I could hear our captain calling out orders, "Full astern, stand by the tubes" and knowing our TGM was trigger happy, I called "What about me?" He yelled: "Keep them off the gun."

My own thoughts at that moment were "Sod the gun, what do I do if the fish hits? Jump for it or what?" The Italian crew looked puzzled but their captain got the idea of the orders and called our captain back alongside. After more arguments in sign language, they agreed to follow *Unshaken* to Malta. Our captain wanted a senior officer from *Menotti* taken on to *Unshaken*. Then he had Lieut. Swanston transferred to the *Menotti* along with Stoker Joe Greenhaugh, who carried a Thompson sub-machine gun. Lieut. Swanston, Joe and I took two on, four off, watching the skipper. On entering *Menotti* we found it by our standards to be dirty and undisciplined. It was steering from aft by hand, making it difficult to steer a straight course. Some time during the day a German bomber was sighted while I was on the bridge with the Italian captain. *Unshaken* dived – the first time I had seen my own ship dive. *Menotti's* captain indicated that he should also dive as the bomber circled. I nodded and stood by the hatch. The captain gave a few orders down the voice pipe, but the bomber made no attempt to attack and made off, so the captain stayed surfaced. I think the defects on *Menotti* were more than just steering.

I later found that when I had jumped on to the casing waving the revolver, it had been unloaded as the bullets were still in the paper packet in my pocket. Joe and I messed in the fore-ends and we had macaroni for every meal. They had a round cheese with this and a grater. I remember Joe and I sitting opposite each other with these huge plates of piled-up macaroni. We muddled our way through the pile until we could see each other and converse once again. We then had a small tin of peaches. I must admit that I was very impressed by these and I have never tasted any to compare with them since. There was also some wine, but I thought it tasted like vinegar.

When *Unshaken* surfaced again we carried on following her to Malta. At dawn the next day Lieut. Swanston and I were on the bridge when Bunting Belson made in semaphore "Good morning, are you all right?" I made back simply "Yes," flags not being my strong point. They closed up and we had a verbal conversation. I requested a shirt, cap and some tea. *Menotti's* officer at this time on *Unshaken* told his crew, who I think were all up there, that he was getting plenty of mungi (food) and they were all envious. When we parted again we kidded the cook to make us some tea. They made it in a coffee pot and it still tasted like coffee. For breakfast that morning the cook broke up some biscuits and poured milky coffee over them. He thought it was cornflakes, but I must admit it tasted very good. The crew of *Menotti* made us feel very welcome and I felt that they were glad it was the end for them. There was no time that I felt at all uneasy with the crew – they spat on Mussolini's picture.

As we were nearing Malta, Lieut. Swanston ordered their ensign to be taken down and ours put up. Joe, Lieut. Swanston and I were on the bridge when suddenly it filled up. They waved their arms about and argued. I said to Joe "Stand by with that machine gun" but the bridge was so crowded that I don't know what would have happened if they hadn't deflated. They tore their flag into 76 pieces and all took one piece of it – a very emotional crew. A trawler came out from Malta with a Maltese crew who could speak Italian, and a couple of TGMs. It was then that Joe and I felt a bit more relaxed and we felt a bit of resentment at the intrusion, for they made the crew withdraw their fish and proceeded to disarm them. It was necessary, of course, but we felt the crew were dejected and really felt quite sorry for them.

We entered harbour and poor old *Menotti* gave up the ghost. The crew got out an old hawser and they were taken in tow, but it broke at the first pull. At this point the Italian fleet came in sight and the crew brightened up considerably. They found an Imperial Italian flag, with a fringe all round it. We three were on the bridge as the boat called alongside to take us off *Menotti.* The captain gave me a pair of binoculars and, I think, a pistol for our captain. He also surrended to Lieut. Swanston a sword, which I believe was returned to him. I saluted him and left for a bath and a rest. During my stay on board *Menotti,* I grew to like and respect the captain, who I felt was shattered by the event.

The facts may not be quite exact but the story is as near as I can remember after all these years.

Twelve Little S Boats

by C.E.R.A. "Skips" Marriott

(This poem was found in the engineroom log book of Sealion. Of the original class of 12, only three – Sealion, Seawolf and Sturgeon – survived the war.)

Twelve little S boats go to it like Bevin,
Starfish goes a bit too far – then there were eleven.

Eleven watchful S boats doing fine and then
Seahorse fails to answer – so there are ten.

Ten stocky S boats in a ragged line,
Sterlet stops and drops out – leaving us nine.

Nine plucky S boats all pursuing fate,
Shark is overtaken – now we are eight.

Eight sturdy S boats – men from Hants and Devon,
Salmon is now overdue – and so the number's seven.

Seven gallant S boats trying all their tricks,
Spearfish tries a newer one – down we come to six.

Six tireless S boats fighting to survive,
No reply from Swordfish so now we tally five.

Five scrubby S boats patrolling close inshore,
Snapper takes a short cut – now we are four.

Four fearless S boats too far out to sea,
Sunfish bombed and scrap-heaped – now we are only three.

Three threadbare S boats patrolling o'er the blue
....
Two icebound S boats..
One lonely S boat ....

A typical S-class interior. This photograph shows Lieut.-Commander Bickford, of H.M.S. Salmon, at the periscope with his First Lieutenant. This class of boat gave rise to the celebrated poem reprinted here. Its unsentimental approach is typical of wartime attitudes.

The nine S boats named as sunk in the above poem were lost as follows:-

STARFISH – Depth-charged in Heligoland Bight, January 20, 1940. Crew survived and were taken P.o.W.

SEAHORSE – Depth-charged in Heligoland Bight, January 7, 1940. Crew of 39 lost.

STERLET – Depth-charged, Skagerrak, April 18, 1940. Crew of 41 lost.

SHARK – Attacked off Norway by aircraft of Luftwaffe. Sunk while being towed by German trawler, July 6, 1940. Survivors were taken P.o.W. (there were two killed and 19 injured).

SALMON – Lost off Norway during July, 1940, probably mined. All 41 crew lost.

SPEARFISH – Sunk by torpedo fired by U34 on August 1, 1940. One survivor, who was taken P.o.W.

SWORDFISH – Mined South of the Isle of Wight with the loss of all 37 crew, November, 1940.

SNAPPER – Lost off Brest February, 1941, with the loss of all 42 crew. Cause of loss not known.

SUNFISH – After being transferred to the Russian Navy, Sunfish was bombed in error by the R.A.F. while en route to Russia. Full crew and British liaison staff all lost.

ABOVE: Ratings from Seraph prepare to hoist their Jolly Roger.

BELOW: Safari enters Portsmouth Harbour and the submarine base at H.M.S. Dolphin, Gosport.

Unbroken

by A. B. John Jones

A group of sailors were standing on the pierhead at H.M.S. Dolphin amid a mass of kitbags, hammocks, suitcases, etc., waiting for a boat to take us across to Vernon steps, where a Royal Navy lorry would transport us to Portsmouth Town Station "en route" to Barrow-in-Furness to join submarine P42, which was nearing completion in Vickers Armstrong yard. Officers, senior ratings and heads of departments had been standing by for the previous six weeks.

I was standing with Geoff McTeare, a dark curly-haired AB whose right arm identified him as a seaman torpedoman. My own right arm bore the asdic badge as I was an AB submarine detector. I had met McTeare at the drafting office when we had been piped to report there, and found we were going on the same draft. We struck up an immediate rapport for he had a sense of humour that was something like my own. Mac had been on one of the old H boats, and I had just left *Sunfish* (which had been bombed on the Tyne) and had volunteered for P42 because my head of department in *Sunfish,* Jan Cryder, Ldg. Tel., H.T.D., was already standing by at Barrow and had asked me to join his new boat.

OK, out pipes! The pierhead officer, a Lieutenant R.N., came out of the office and the crew of the picket boat made their way down the stone steps to the boat that was tied alongside. The Lieutenant read out our names and when he was assured we were all present we were ordered to embark. Carrying our gear we boarded the boat for the first stage of our journey to Barrow.

The train was crowded but we had a carriage reserved for the draft so we felt privileged as we sat there and ate our packed lunches and watched the Hampshire countryside roll past the window. On arrival at Waterloo we were herded to another R.N. transport for the trip across London to Euston (or was it Kings Cross?) At Euston we found we had a two-hour wait for the train. The killick in charge of the draft told us not to wander too far away, to have a drink if we felt like it but on no account miss the train. Mac and I found a nice little pub not far from the station and sat down to enjoy a few pints. Four or five pints later and in the mood for a convivial evening we decided that the war could get on for another day without the services of these two particular ABs, and having decided that, we made off for the bright lights of the big city. Suffice to say we got drunk and enjoyed a night of horizontal refreshment with two ladies of the night.

The next morning, after a breakfast in the station buffet, we inquired about trains to Barrow and found there was one pretty early, so we presented ourselves at the R.T.O.'s office and said we had missed our draft and had no travel documents as the killick in charge of the party had the warrant. He gave us a right ticking off, and after inquiries had been made, he issued us with a travel warrant and the hope that "we got our arses kicked from here to breakfast time, and enough stoppage of leave to keep us on board for years to come."

When we got to Barrow, we made our way to Vickers yard and asked where P42 was lying. We were directed to the ship's office, a wooden structure, and on knocking the door were bade to enter. A small bald-headed C.P.O. sat behind the desk. This was the coxswain, Joe Sizer. When we reported who we were he said: "You two are right in it. We were due to do a basin dive this morning, but because you two decided to bag off we hadn't a full crew and the dive had to be put off. You are already in the rattle and will see the skipper in the morning, but first you'll see Jimmy and I can assure you he's in a foul mood over your behaviour." Telling us to stay where we were he vanished into the inner office. After about five minutes, he told us we would see Jimmy now, so, into the office, Caps Off, and we are stood in front of Lieut. Taylor, R.N.R., our new first lieutenant. He was a stout, dark-haired man dressed in a ragged officer's jacket with two frayed rings on each sleeve. He glared up at us balefully and then let us have it in no uncertain terms and said if it was up to him we would spend the rest of the war doing "Number Elevens." Turning to the coxswain he snapped: "Captain's Report." On caps, about turn, we were marched out of the office.

"You had better see about digs" said the 'swain. "I have a list here, see if any of them can put you up and report back here at 0800 tomorrow morning." We found digs at 35, Manchester Street, with a Mrs. Lacey, a good-hearted lady and, as we found out, a very good cook. Her husband worked in the yard and they had one son, Billy, who was twelve years old. We felt at home right away and it was a pleasant interlude to be fussed after by this kind lady, but at the back of our minds was the encounter with the captain.

The next morning we reported to the yard and with some apprehension awaited the call to "Captain's Table." We had not long to wait. "MacTeare, Jones" the coxswain barked, "Quick march! Halt! Off Caps!" We halted in front of the desk and got our first glimpse of the Captain, Lieutenant Alistair Campbell Gillespie Mars, R.N. He sat grim-faced while the coxswain read out the charge against us: "Did wilfully miss the draft, 24 hours adrift" etc. "Well what do you have to say in answer to these charges?" he said. Mac told the story of how we had got lost and must have just missed the train by a minute or so and then it was my turn to answer the charges so I said "It was just as Able Seaman MacTeare stated it." Mars sat back in his chair and said in a very cold voice "You two have put the Royal Navy and Vickers Armstrong to a great deal of trouble, two sailors who have caused the cancellation of a very important basin dive for your own selfish pleasures. What do you plead?"

We both pleaded guilty and were awarded ten days' stoppage of leave, which could not be implemented because we were living ashore, but Mars assured us that until it could be implemented he would see to it that we would work our fingers to the bone. He was as good as his word, for when we did the belated basin dive MacTeare and I carried tons of pig iron from for'ard to aft and from aft to for'ard till I thought we would drop from exhaustion. Any dirty job that had to be done, Mac and I were there to do it.

Even on social occasions we were not let off the hook. A dance was arranged for the crew, Vickers personnel and landladies to thank them for their efforts. Mac and I had to be at the hall early to "dress" it with bunting and balloons, act as barmen and when the dance was finished, sweep up and remove the decorations, so while the rest of the crew were wooing the fair lasses of Barrow we were pulling our plum out. Mrs. Lacey was indignant that her two well-behaved lodgers should be treated in such a way and it took all our powers of persuasion to keep her from telling Mars so. So here ends the sorry saga of how Mac and I joined the P42, hardly a good beginning to the commission.

After basin dives and various other trials we were ready for leaving Barrow. I had acquainted myself with my part of the ship as the asdic set was a different type to what I had been used to on *Sunfish,* where it had been a type 120. Now on P42 we had a type 129, which had the oscillator fitted as a part of the keel. On *Sunfish* we had to raise and lower the oscillator and it was the devil's own job to do it by hand, which we had to do as part of routine maintenance. It took 2,000 turns to lower it and the same to raise it.

As well as my A/S duties I was casing party. The second coxswain, John (Cock) Goodwin, took me under his wing as we were known to each other from the *Sunfish.* Cock was ancient in my eyes (he must have been at least forty years old for he had been outside for quite a few years after doing his time and was recalled at the start of hostilities as a Royal Fleet Reservist). He had helped me a great deal when I was passing out as an able seaman. A cockney with a craggy face and a very droll sense of humour, he kept doling out little snippets of seamanship to me as we went about our work on the casing. Other members of the casing party were MacTeare, Bramhall, Butterworth, and the after casing party was Fenton, our gunlayer, Mullet, the other A/S rating, and Laidler.

The Petty Officers' Mess consisted of Coxswain Joe Sizer, Tancy Lee, the Torpedo Gunner's Mate, John Willey, the P.O. Telegraphist, and Fred Sharp, the Stoker P.O. The E.R.A.s' mess housed the three tiffies, Chief E.R.A. Mick Manuel, a tall lean Irishman, Howard Lewis, the Outside E.R.A., a small dark-haired Welshman, and Ted Lewis, a Londoner.

This brings me to the wardroom. As I've said, I had already met the Captain across the table as soon as I'd joined the boat, but as I saw him going about the boat in these busy days I came to realise what an efficient and capable officer he was, and saw how he got the dockyard people to rectify certain little things that weren't to his liking. He wasn't very tall, with wavy brown hair, boyish good looks, face scrubbed pink and always smartly dressed, even in white overalls which he wore about the dockyard. His prim and proper appearance soon earned him the nickname "Pansy." Jimmy, Lieut. Taylor, I just couldn't take to. He was a frustrated thespian who was forever playing the Hollywood version of the swashbuckling submarine officer. He was tubby and there was an Andrews Sister record that was very popular at the time called "Boogly Woogly Piggy," so Jimmy soon got the nickname Boogly Woogly. Lieut. John Haddow, the navigator and armaments officer, was a very tall thin Scot, who was quickly christened "Diprod." Sub-Lieut. Paul Thirsk, a tall fair-haired reserve officer, completed the Wardroom personnel.

Came the day when we were to leave Barrow and proceed to join the depot ship *Forth* in Holy Loch. It was blustery as we steamed out of Barrow into the Irish Sea, where our escort *H.M.S. Cutty Sark* was standing off. On the passage to the Clyde we carried out crash dives and deep diving trials and except for a few small leaks here and there, which the dockyard mateys took note of, we were perfectly all right for sea-going duties. I believe the actual signing over of the boat from dockyard to Admiralty hands was recommended by the skipper in the wardroom on passage. I was on the wheel, heaving into a bucket.

Alongside *H.M.S. Forth* the faults found on passage were speedily put right by the dockyard mateys, who then took off for home, leaving us to be welded into an efficient submarine crew. Each day we would carry out trials of some sort in the loch, speed trials, or refuelling from a tanker whilst steaming round the loch. This latter took place in a blinding snowstorm and I can remember the numbing cold as we stood on the casing and pulled the fuel pipe from the tanker to the boat, pulling hand over hand on a wet freezing rope till our hands were chafed and blue, then huddling in the shelter of the bridge till the fuelling was completed. We did diving trials to see how fast we could get to periscope depth. Again and again we carried out this operation till at last Mars was grudgingly satisfied with our performance. (It was to stand us in good stead in the future).

The ten days' stoppage of leave awarded to MacTeare and me was now in effect, so while the rest of the crew were able to go ashore and sample the delights of bonny Dunoon we had extra work to do on board and what time we had to ourselves was spent in the "Goffer Bar." It was hell listening to them when they came aboard late at night, pissed up and with tales of conquests over the local lassies. It was then I pulled my "con" trick over Their Lordships. One day AB Mullet (the other A/S rating) and I were told we were to report to the Asdic School ashore at Dunoon for a course in new asdic procedure. We were to catch the 0800 boat ashore each morning and report back aboard *Forth* when classes were over on each of the three days that the course lasted. This meant we were victualled for dinner in the Asdic School for the three days. On the first morning we duly reported to the regulating office of the establishment and presenting our papers, were victualled in. The R.P.O. asked if we were TG or UA. With all the assurance of a three-badged AB, I answered "Grog." As we left the office Mullet said to me "You'll get f....g shot." The outcome of it was that for three days I stood in line at tot time and drew my ration of "Nelson's Blood" and I'm sure those three tots must have been the nicest I ever drank. I was never found out – I'm sure the Admiralty had bigger things on their minds than three tots of Two in One.

We left *Forth* one morning for Loch Long to do torpedo trials and it was a quiet pleasant interlude. Each day after trials we would gather in the "snug" of the Arrochar Hotel, drink our ale and have a sing-song with the locals. It was still very cold and snowy and I remember one of us remarking how cold the beer was to the teeth. One of the old fellows in the snug took the poker, stuck it into the blazing fire then plunged it into the beer. It warmed the beer and also gave it a tang, so from then on we were all confirmed "mullers." We had a dance in a hall behind the hotel just before leaving and this time I was able to take part in the festivities, dancing wild highland schottisches with a brawny Scots lass who flung me around as if I was a paperweight, (which indeed I was).

Torpedo tube trials over, it was back to *Forth.* Buzzes spread as to when we were going to sea and to where, charts were taken on board and the guesses began. Most turned out correct. Came the day we were to sail and we stored ship and had our last meal inboard. It was a memorable one, and just as a final fling and for the sheer hell of it we had a "Yankee Dish-up" and left the rest of the mess deck wondering what hit them.

At 1300 we fell in at harbour stations and slipped our moorings. With "Good Luck" cries ringing in our ears we sailed towards the mouth of Holy Loch, out past Aila Craig and into the Irish Sea. P42 was in all respects ready to play her part in the war.

Trooper

Extracts from the diaries of E.R.A. Peter Forbes

November 5, 1942. Left Dunoon to do trial runs with our new inventions, two-man torpedoes.

November 12. Left for Malta, no stops on the way, where we are to operate from to do our "jeep" runs as we call them. Immediately we got under way the captain told us that these jeeps had had a successful attack on the *Tirpitz* in a Norwegian fiord.

November 14. Hugging the coast on the surface, we must be near Lands End now. Still on the surface although the escort has left us. The trip is to take us 14 days.

November 15. Dived all day today as we are within range of the enemy now. Had a practice alarm last night. All's well, but I miss Molly very much.

November 16. My birthday today, 24 now, getting old.

November 17. RDF has fallen over, we were relying a lot on it, too. It may take us longer as we were planning to do three days on the surface, but must dive all day now.

November 19. A week out, now in the danger area. It is said to be infested with U-boats.

November 20. We are in Portuguese waters now, close to shore. We saw the lights of Lisbon last night. Liable to be interned if we are caught. Ahead of schedule so going slow.

November 21. Still on dive routine all day. Our fresh food is nearing exhaustion so we will have to revert to dehydrated foodstuffs now. Crash dive last night, enemy aircraft about.

November 23. Escort took us past Gibraltar. We were dived to avoid our tanks (in which we carry the jeeps) being seen.

November 28. Nothing has happened so far, touch wood. We dived through an enemy minefield near Pantellaria, an Italian fortified island near Malta. It's safe to dive through minefields ordinarily but with tanks on it is very dangerous. Miss Molly so much, was thinking how awful it would be never to see her again.

November 29. Dived through half of a minefield, then at night the captain decided to charge at full speed on top of the minefield the rest of the night. Our luck held through. Thank God.

November 30. Arrived Malta. Glad to get a real drop of fresh air and to see the outside world again. Malta is in a terrible state of ruin. The people there have stood up to the enemy's bombardment magnificently. Food is in very short supply, too. During our stay in Malta we will be doing trial runs almost daily with our jeeps. We are all wondering what harbour we are going into. We assume it is to sink units of the Italian Fleet in harbour.

Christmas day in Malta wasn't too bad but it was still the worst I have ever had, my third away from home. Went to Communion in the morning. Our sister ship, *Traveller,* went on a trial for us in Taranto harbour to see if she could stay on the surface there for an hour as we have to do. It couldn't have been possible as she hasn't returned, given up for lost. This sort of thing dampens our spirits.

December 27. Left Malta to do our secret job with our two-man torpedoes. Three submarines fitted out the same as us, we are all going to the same place, we think.

December 29. Our aim is to enter Palermo Bay and attack shipping in the port, which is on the North coast of Sicily and is the starting point for supply runs to North Africa (Tripoli).

December 31. Last day of the year. Sighted an Italian convoy, easy target, but the captain has his orders to leave everything alone as we are after bigger game. We are close to Sicily now. Was thinking what Molly will be doing at midnight.

January 1, 1943. Entered the bay last night at 2100. Surfaced nearly three miles from port. Sat on the surface and sent off the jeeps. This took us nearly an hour. Two submarines were there, us and *Thunderbolt.* The third boat was sent to attack a port in Sardinia. We set off again at full speed on the donkeys (main diesels).

January 4. According to reports we sank a cruiser and five ships between us.

January 7. After a few more days of suspense, we finally arrive back in Malta. Six letters waiting for me. All from Molly.

January 9. A few of the men on the jeeps were killed, the two of us returned safely, but the one that attacked the other port hasn't returned, presumed lost. Another "T" boat. During our short stay in Malta, six submarines have been lost in the Mediterranean. The trouble is that summer is coming on and the water is then very clear and you can be spotted by aircraft at a good depth.

February 3. Left Malta for a 14-day patrol. Our captain is in hospital so we have a temporary replacement.

February 4. Our patrol is to be off the coast of Greece to the toe of Italy. Supposed to be a quiet billet. This skipper is supposed to be no good according to the know-alls.

February 6. On our billet now, plenty of enemy aircraft about. Have to go deep to avoid them. The captain seems to be efficient, though.

February 7. Plenty of schooners about. Small things, too small to waste a torpedo on and too dangerous to go to gun action against them.

February 9. Sighted a 9,000-ton vessel coming out of an Albanian port. Full speed ahead towards it to get ready to attack it, when lo and behold a Red Cross began to make itself clear on the ship's side, a hospital ship, what a let-down. Many of us are of the opinion to sink it (we are a bloodthirsty crew). For all we knew it may be full of troops. Left it to go unmolested on its way.

February 10. Have been watching a railway bridge on the mainland all day. Plenty of long trains have crossed it, we may go to gun action to wreck it. Risky job, though. Four months married today.

February 12. Working our way up the coast, nothing of any size yet. Plenty of aircraft about, though.

February 13. Off the island of Corfu. Chased three small ships on

H.M. Submarine Trooper during working-up trials in Scotland. She carried out operations at Palermo with human torpedoes, and after a brief but successful career, was reported missing in October, 1943. She was probably mined in the Leros area of the Mediterranean.

the surface last night but they escaped us in the darkness and a mist that sprang up. Plenty of enemy aircraft flying around us so we expect a convoy to pass us tomorrow. The aircraft will be clearing the way for it – they hope.

February 14. At noon we sighted an Italian destroyer coming out of one of the ports. As we were three miles out we went into a position it must pass to attack it. A few moments later a large supply ship, about 6,000 tons, came out so the captain decided to try to sink the supply ship, then if we had time, have a go at the destroyer. A few anxious moments of suspense while the enemy drew nearer and we waited to let go our tubes of destruction. The moment came and we fired four torpedoes at the supply ship which had turned out to be a naval depot ship, a good prize. Then fired two fish at the destroyer. We heard three hits out of the first salvo then we dived to 150 feet to avoid depth charges. We shut off for depth-charging. Immediately we were surrounded by explosions that came nearer. It's not a very pleasant feeling, either, looking at the ship's side, thinking that it might bulge in at any moment. However our captain, by careful dodging, managed to draw further away from the destroyer, which we must have missed. We counted 45 depth charges. We came back to periscope depth and saw wreckage floating about so the depot ship must have sunk. The destroyer had raced back to port, we presume to get more depth charges, so we decided to go to a safe position till it blows over.

February 16. On our way back to Malta. Had to put the ASDIC rating in the captain's report for sleeping on watch. We were at 60 feet dodging the enemy aircraft and can't use the periscope below 30 feet, so the asdic rating is the ears of the boat. All our lives are in his hands and I for one want to see my wife again. This rating had been noticed before dozing at his post.

February 17. Molly's birthday today. Hope she got the flowers I had arranged for her to receive. I wish I were with her today of all days.

February 18. Arrived back in Malta with the Jolly Roger flying at our mast. We were in dry dock for a clean-up and a few jobs had to be done to the engines. Bought Molly some pyjamas and silk stockings which I will keep until I get home (if I ever do). Three more British submarines have been lost lately. It seems to come in spells, you may have a good run of luck then the bad has to come.

March 4. Left Malta to do a long patrol, our last from Malta as we will finish up in Algiers at the end of this one.

March 5. Three years in the Navy today. This patrol is going to last nearly twenty days. We are to operate in the Straits of Messina between Italy and Sicily. Ten of our submarines are to act as a sort of wolfpack.

March 6. Sighted three merchant ships escorted by four destroyers, fired two torpedoes which were seen by the enemy so we had to break off the attack and dive for our lives. Needless to say the enemy avoided our torpedoes. Then followed merry hell let loose. Explosions all round us, but not near enough to cause us any major worries. Our captain is very good.

March 8. Working our way up the coast of Italy, six miles off the shore during the day then at night surface some distance out and charge our batteries up.

March 9. Nothing but small fishing smacks sailing around. Have a look at the shore through the periscope and you can see quite plainly the little villages and many ruins of castles and churches. Received a W/T message to get in a position to attack a convoy of four merchant vessels and six destroyers that is making its way to Tunisia. Tried to cover the distance in time but the enemy had passed through our billet and may be attacked by the submarine on the next billet. Attacking an escort of six destroyers is an ambitious move. Another message to lay in wait off Cape Mayillo on the north coast of Sicily to meet a convoy which is expected to leave the harbour soon.

March 10. Stopped our engines at 2300 last night to listen in the stillness of the night for any noise from the convoy. No signs and at 0500 we dived just as dawn was breaking. We thought we had missed it but at 1600, just as we were having tea, the captain sighted a convoy of three merchant vessels with an escort of three destroyers. We attacked one of the m/v's, firing two torpedoes. They hit the ship and a destroyer came racing towards us and the captain fired two torpedoes at her but she dodged them and immediately dropped a shower of depth charges. They were the nearest yet and it wasn't a pleasant experience at all. At the first one our lucky horseshoe fell off its hook. The noise of the depth charges gradually grew fainter until they ceased at about 2100, five hours after our attack began. We stayed down until midnight, then surfaced to charge up our batteries. Five months married.

March 11. Quiet day. We are about 120 miles away from yesterday's attack. Received signal to go back as there is another convoy that has been sighted by the R.A.F.

March 12. Back to that area to wait for convoy, which consists of four m/v's, four destroyers and six E-boats – a well-guarded convoy.

We sighted it and tried to get into position for attack but they picked up our motors on their asdic gear and dropped a pattern of charges. A near thing for us.

March 15. At periscope depth the sea is like a mirror, calm, and the periscope can be seen miles away; very hard to attack under these conditions. At 2030 the night alarm went and we all went to our action stations. Order to get torpedoes ready; big convoy up top. We fired four torpedoes, two at a large troopship of about 10,000 tons and two at a destroyer. The convoy was about four miles away but we heard three hits, very good play on the captain's part. We immediately dived expecting a shower of depth charges but we only got two near ones. They dropped no more so the troopship must have sunk and they were picking up survivors. Very lucky for us.

March 16. Quiet day for us. Sighted three destroyers, tried to attack them but they were moving too fast away from us to reach them. Plenty of wreckage about after last night. This is proving a very lively patrol area. Plenty of enemy ships, in fact too many for our comfort. Never mind, every ship we sink is estimated to save 10,000 of our "Tommies" in Tunisia.

March 17. Looking for another convoy; six ships, no details. 1030, action stations. Sighted three m/v's and three destroyers. Full speed attack under water, periscope depth. Fired three fish at an m/v then the captain calmly fired another three at a destroyer. We immediately dived deep. Heard two hits off first salvo then one hit off the second salvo. The destroyer was a fast-moving target. About 20 depth charges dropped fairly near us. It's an awful sensation waiting for the charges to go off, never knowing whether the next one has our name on it. Suddenly they broke off the counter-attack – picking up survivors again? We gradually come sliding up to the surface again. Up periscope and see one of the destroyers alongside a sinking m/v taking off survivors, so fired a couple of fish at her. She saw the tracks and came racing towards us. A crash dive and the destroyer just missed cutting us in two. Our hearts were in our mouths as her turbines were so close they sounded like a train in a tunnel. Then followed a couple of hours of more bangs than that. But we finally escaped, thank God.

March 18. We have only three stern torpedoes left now. We have got another signal giving us the position of another convoy; two troopships and five destroyers. It must have been valuable, so big an escort, but it is a good distance away. We hope to see it, though, to bring our bag of victims up. We leave the billet for Algiers tonight. We never met the convoy. On our way home to base we were attacked by Italian bombers while charging our batteries. They missed, though.

March 21. Arrived safely in Algiers today. First mail for nearly three months, 50 letters in all, 28 from Molly. They expect a big raid tonight as a big convoy of seven large m/v's, luxury liner transporters. One of them is being towed in, the convoy was attacked for days on end on its way from England but they beat them off. Good old Navy.

March 25. Anniversary of our engagement. Happy memories. A big air raid. I had been ashore with two of my mess mates and had a bottle of champagne to celebrate. We rowed off in the middle of the raid, shrapnel and bullets dropping all around in the water. But we are full of dutch courage and don't care for those b. . . . Germans. Came on board and had a few minutes of firing the Lewis gun at imaginary planes. The sky was lit up with tracer bullets and searchlights. It was fun. One ship in the harbour was sunk and plenty of near misses. Next morning – oh, my head. Beating like a kettle drum.

I had a few walks ashore here and found many beautiful spots, lovely gardens where all kinds of animals and fish were. While we were here, three of our class were due but never arrived. They had been following us up in each billet, as we left another came up and so on. So we are all wondering if our class are too big for the Med. Too easily seen. Submarine Rear Admiral flies here from London to hold a conference about it. Then he gives a speech – the usual tale of how proud he is of us, how the country is proud of us. But those three boats were with us at Malta and we used to know each other very well. Meeting at the E.R.A.s' club ashore and having good times together and it makes you very morbid to think that they will never return, our buddies. And the worst of it is our submarine caused so much havoc in those billets before them that they must have been waiting to sink them. We are literally murderers.

The outcome of the conference was that "T" boats have to carry on. The supplies to Tunisia must be destroyed no matter what the cost. We were promised a quiet billet next patrol just to prove that "T" boats come back. Proper Navy wangling. Three boats lost were *Turbulent, Tigress* and *Thunderbolt (ex-Thetis). Thunderbolt* was one of the three jeepers, so that leaves only us fitted to use the two-man torpedoes. Never mind, if I survive this war I can say I have done my little bit in it.

April 5, 1943. Left Algiers for patrol, a promised quiet billet. Before we left the Admiral came aboard and wished us good luck and a safe return, gave us flattering compliments on our last patrol, too.

April 8. On our billet now, still nothing doing. Have seen plenty of aircraft transports (Italian) on their way to Tunisia.

April 10. Too quiet to be true. Hitler must be leaving Rommel's troops to their doom as we are patrolling between Sardinia and Sicily. Last night we heard the R.A.F. bombing the ports of Sicily. We dived to get out of the way of bombers in case they had seen us.

April 13. Still very quiet. Sighted five destroyers today sweeping a channel for a convoy. They heard us moving about and came over and tried to pick us up again, but we were in silent routine at 120 feet. They went away so we came up again, but two hours later we saw them again. This time they picked us up on their asdics and gave us a heavy dose of depth charging. Nothing damaged, a few lamps bust.

April 15. Dived last night to avoid bombing by enemy aircraft, who dropped flares and saw us charging our batteries. Today we saw three destroyers but they were too far away.

April 18. Billet is very quiet indeed, nothing happening at all so far. We don't worry, though, we need a good rest.

April 19. Sighted two destroyers escorting an m/v. Went to action stations and we crept nearer to deliver our fish of death to the enemy. Fired three torpedoes at the m/v but the tracks were seen by the destroyer, who came racing towards us, so we crash dived to 150 feet. We heard two of our torpedoes hitting the m/v and then a proper load of depth charges came tumbling down on us, shaking us up properly.

The crew of H.M. Submarine Trump crowd the casing to display their Jolly Roger in the final year of the war.

Too near to be any comfort. About thirty dropped, all very near us. We were all praying hard. The captain was calmly sitting listening on the asdics to the engines of the destroyer, giving orders to the helmsman to alter course away from them. Suddenly the charges stopped, then was a quietness, you can't realise the stillness of everyone. We were afraid to breathe even in case the enemy would hear us. The captain said "Their engines have stopped now. They must be picking up survivors." We gradually crept silently away from the scene of destruction. A tot of rum was issued all round. We needed it.

April 20. We should have left our billet last night to return to Algiers but the R.A.F. bombed Naples very heavily and the Italian fleet decided to find another safer port, so we received a signal to intercept it. We hope it changes course. The fleet consists of two battleships, two cruisers, eight destroyers and 20 "E" boats. What a hope of getting away if we sink any of it. We are now looking hard for it.

April 21. The fleet altered course before it reached us and we are on our way back. We are glad we missed it, though. Hope to receive a lot of mail when we get in.

April 23. Arrived in Algiers again after a fairly quiet patrol. Only very old mail waiting for us, Christmas mail!! Met an old pal of mine here, "Doodles" Robertson. Had a good time talking to him.

April 28. Some more bad news for our flotilla. Three more submarines have been lost: *Sahib, Regent* and *Splendid.* All pals of ours, too. We must be a very lucky boat, or our captain must be the best of them. It is a very morbid mess on our depot ship, watching the gear of our old buddies being packed away and out of their lockers to go home to be sold as dead-men's effects.

May 1. We had a visit here of the *Nelson, Rodney,* two cruisers and 20 destroyers. They must be waiting for the enemy's evacuation of Tunis.

May 5. We heard good news of some of our pals on the wireless tonight. Only three members of the crew of *Sahib* have been lost, the rest are PoW's. We are all glad they are alive anyway. Their loved ones at home will be glad of the news.

May 9. We should have left Algiers tonight to go on patrol but our sailing was cancelled at the last moment. We are leaving this flotilla now that Tunisia is ours and we are going to the other end of the Med.

May 10. Seven months married today. Left Algiers on passage to Malta. We are taking all our spare gear and some supplies to Malta. We don't know where we go from there. The journey should take us about a week.

May 13. On passage. All Tunisia is now ours and we shall be the first submarine to pass the coast there for some time as it has been patrolled by cruisers and destroyers. Submarines played the biggest part in stopping supplies reaching Rommel. Very quiet journey.

May 16. Still very quiet. Passed Pantellaria at night on the surface, but the R.A.F. had bombed it very heavily yesterday. Arrive in Malta tomorrow morning.

May 17. Arrived Malta but we will only stay a few days. Glad to meet some of our old pals. They all thought we had been sunk, and we were feeding the fishes. A grand feeling to have returned from the dead.

May 21. A raid early in the morning by enemy planes but they never reached here – our fighters drove them off. The defence guns shot down one raider. They were trying for the convoy that arrived at dawn this morning. Many alerts were sounded today but our fighters kept them at bay.

May 22. We leave here tomorrow on patrol and to land commandos somewhere. We finish up in Syria.

May 23. Left Malta to do a secret operation with commandos. We land them on an island off the coast of Greece, called Zante, and pick them up again next night. We then steam up the coast of Italy, where we land them again. They are going to land stores for some future plan.

May 25. We did the job last night. We went within a mile of the island on our motors and stopped, put off two canoes, one empty and being towed by the other one contining an officer and a corporal. The object was to land, damage one of the canoes, put stale sandwiches and empty beer bottles in it and leave it there. There is some vast idea behind it all. We think it is to give the enemy a scare and something to keep them busy when they find it. We dropped them at 2200 and went out for a couple of hours. We returned in and picked up the men, using pre-arranged signals, then steamed out at full speed. The objective of the operation was a success. Anniversary today.

May 27. On our way to do the other job. We are passing through very dangerous waters today, it is a very narrow channel taking us into the Adriatic Sea. Very heavily mined but our luck is holding so far. We saw a ship in the channel but the captain decided to leave it alone as we have no scope to dodge the escorts. We are the first British submarine to enter the Adriatic since January: then it was beginning to get too dangerous. This afternoon we heard wires scraping along the hull. It's a nerve-wracking moment, waiting for the explosion that you won't hear. The silence in the boat is deadly and you can cut it with a knife. The captain managed to get us out of the danger. He is very good. We would follow him anywhere.

May 30. Cruising about two or three miles off the east coast of Italy at a place called Vieste, where we land the commandos tomorrow night.

May 30. Carefully watching the coastline to find a suitable place to land. It is a little bay with a sandy beach. Tonight we intend going within a mile from the shore. We shall be in water with a depth of only 60 feet.

May 31. At 2100 we went into this little bay on the surface to within a mile and a half, opened the forehatch and got the two canoes out and eight big watertight tins of explosives and a transmitting and receiving wireless set. The commandos set sail for shore and we steamed out to a safer position to charge our batteries. We returned at 0200 and picked up the commandos again. We have previously agreed on a code of signals as it was very dark. The object was to land the explosives and dig a hole to hide them, marking the spot with pieces of Malta rock that had been taken for the purpose. Our secret service men ashore could then take the explosives to do sabotage work. It was a complete success. As we were in the bay a patrol boat passed quite close to us so we stopped all our machinery till she passed. We were expecting their searchlight to play on us, then the shore batteries would have had a sitting target to fire upon.

June 1. We went to action stations at 0530. In the coming dawn the captian saw a dark shape. It grew lighter and he saw an 800-ton tanker escorted by a destroyer. It was like a sheet of glass, the surface of the water, so the skipper didn't think it worth the risk to sink it as they were bound to see the tracks of the torpedoes. Our captain is a very sound man, not one of those "Daily Mirror" captains who take all sorts of daft risks just to get their name in the papers. Those captains show no regard for the value of their crew's lives. One day our new Jimmy asked the captain if he would attack a lone destroyer. The captain replied "You might, but I value my wife and family too much to do such a daft thing."

June 2. Action stations at the same time again off the naval port of Bari. The range was ten miles, a big merchantman, too far away. We saw four ships all taking the same course hugging the coast but there's a minefield between us and the narrow channel so we continue to watch this channel, plotting the position of it on our charts. The captain is going to try to get in this channel by tomorrow morning. We leave our billet tomorrow for port, which is a new base for us, Beirut.

June 3. Dived at dawn, 0345. All expecting to go to action stations shortly. But we never saw a thing even though we were only six miles off the entrance to Bari. We were sitting down to tea at 1600 saying it was just our luck, good or bad, to miss seeing any ships, when action stations went. A ship had come out of the harbour. We went in to 3,000 yards and fired four torpedoes. During the attack we kept hitting patches of fresh water being so near the shore and we had difficulty in keeping an even trim. Just as we fired, the boat gave a dip forward and we went from 30 to 70 feet before we stopped. We waited for the explosions saying we had hit but none came. The torpedoes must have been diverted from their course when we dipped. We came up to periscope depth to try to get another salvo of fish at her but she had steamed safely out of range. The best of it was the escort didn't even see the tracks of the torpedoes, so we escaped a spell of depth charging, thank goodness.

June 4. Passing through the narrow mined channel out of the Adriatic. Sorry the captain missed yesterday but he is blaming no one. It was just one of those things.

June 5. On our way down the coast of Albania and Greece. Last night we sent a signal to Malta telling of our successful commando trips. We were at 70 feet all day, it was very rough up top.

June 7. Passing Crete on our way to Beirut. The past week we have been on very low water rations. One gallon per man per day for all uses. And our food is low, one loaf between eight of us per day. Glad to get in port to get a decent meal.

June 10. Another month of married life gone by. We struck a bit of wreckage last night and it seems to have bent our port propeller. Still diving by day.

June 13. Arrived at Beirut at 0800. Having been on very short rations for a fortnight we were very glad to get a good meal when we arrived. The day before we arrived we were afforded the luxury of a bath. First one since we left Malta. We needed it. Were congratulated on our success with the commandos.

June 16. This is the best base the Navy has. An old barracks, the very best of everything. Pictures every night and an ice cream bar. Plenty of fruit here. The first time we have seen bananas for years. Working tropical routine to get repairs done to our machinery. Expect to be a fortnight in harbour, then on to Port Said to go into dry dock to have our spare propeller fitted.

June 21. Have just spent three days up at Alley, the rest camp for submarine crews. A lovely place 3,800 feet up from the sea, in a mountain. In the morning you get a clear view down to the sea. We are far above the level of the barrage balloons. At night we are in cloud and mist.

One day we took a trip by bus to Damascus, the oldest city in the world standing today. The road climbed to a height of 6,500 feet twisting and turning, then, far below, we saw a flat fertile plain; the Plains of Lebanon. Then came the journey down, the driver had his gears in all the time. We rounded sharp corners seeing a sheer drop from the road. Not a drive for a weak person. A few army convoys passed us on the way and a mule train was seen in the mountains. Lovely rugged countryside. In the valley the people still used primitive methods with their ground, cutting the crops with a hand knife and putting it in stacks by hand. The plough is only a bit of wood, one handle, pulled by a camel or a bullock. We passed an Armenian village with its mud huts with a mosque in the centre. The mule is still the means of transport used by the Arabs. We then climbed out of the valley again up tortuous bends to 5,000 feet. Above us we could see snow-capped mountains. They must have been very high because we were sweltering in the heat.

Just before we arrived at Damascus we passed about ten miles of barren land, just like the wilderness mentioned in the Bible. Damascus itself has its two contrasts, the old and the new. The old contains all the mosques and bazaars, with the natives beating out silverware by hand. They also weave silk, all by hand. Not having much time we couldn't go into many places. The new architecture is lovely, the city has its different quarters; Jewish, Moslem, Arab, Greek and of course the white colony. Most of the women wore veils over their faces.

The journey back was in the cool of evening and as we climbed up the mountains we were in the clouds and mist, proving very chilly. We arrived back at the rest camp tired and hungry but a big meal was waiting for us. It had been a very interesting journey. Those three days' rest were the first we have had since we left home, so we deserved it. The patrols out here are no picnic. Our stay in Beirut was very nice indeed – a nice clean bed to sleep in at night with a mosquito net over it, and plenty of food. The shops are full of unrationed goods and clothes but the prices are extortionate, far above our rate of pay.

June 30. Left Beirut on our way to Port Said to enter dock for a minor refit and a new propeller to be fitted. A two-day run, dived all day.

July 2. Arrived Port Said, entered floating dock. Very warm with no water around us, the sun beats down on the shell and it's like an oven, but the work must be done so, wearing singlet and shorts, we nearly sweat drops of blood. No wonder I an growing thin.

July 3. I had a walk ashore and this place is like all other cities I have seen out here. The native part is terrible while the fashionable part is very nice. We stayed at an old hotel, Southways, converted into a barracks. Nice view right on the main street. Went to the pictures, open air.

July 4. Entered hospital, collapsed in Southways, temperature and pain in the stomach. Suspected appendix. Terrible pain.

July 7. Came out of hospital, still shaky but we leave for patrol tomorrow so I must catch the boat or else I may be kept here for years.

July 8. Left Port Said for a long patrol. Do two days on the surface as the area has been swept clean and they say we have supreme air superiority here.

July 9. On our way to the Adriatic for a 23-day patrol. A big offensive is in the wind so we may be diverted or caught right in the middle of it. While we were at Port Said 15 large troopships came through the canal, American, British, Dutch and Norwegian. They left again next day for some port in the Med. Some pushing-off point, we presume. We have a new captain. Our own captain has been left in Beirut to undergo an operation. This one is suspected to be wild devil. We don't want him taking any stupid risks just to make a name for himself.

July 10. We sighted aircraft yesterday and set up a flare. It proved to be an Italian so we had to crash dive, then he just missed us with his bombs. But a miss is as good as a mile, so all's well. Dive all day tomorrow.

July 11. Heard of invasion of Sicily, rejoiced at the good news. We are working up the coast of Greece on our way to the coast of Albania in the Adriatic, where it is reputed to be very heavily mined. Nothing unusual, everywhere we go it seems to be mined.

July 12. Sighted a destroyer and A/S boat cruising around outside a port on the island of Zante. Went to diving stations expecting an m/v to come out after a channel had been swept, but we waited in vain for an hour, so we went back to normal routine patrolling up and down six miles off the mouth of the harbour.

July 13. Normal day at periscope depth passing through the straits into the Adriatic.

July 14. At 0800 we went to diving stations to attack a 3,000-ton m/v off Cape Durazzo on the coast of Albania. We fired three torpedoes, all missed, so the captain decided to go to gun action to sink or damage it. Surfaced and got three rounds fired when shore batteries opened fire on us. We carried on firing, getting a few hits on the target then a shell flew through the casing just missing the pressure hull by inches. By this time two other ships had come on the scene and they, too, were letting fly at us. This proved too much for us so we had to dive out of the way.

We kept at periscope depth and the last the captain saw of the m/v was that it had gone on to some rocks and was burning fiercely aft. The action had only lasted a few moments by the clock but it seemed ages, all the time expecting a shell to come tearing through the control

Two aspects of life in T-class boats, always popular with their crews because of their good and solid construction. ABOVE: Truant's crew proudly display their Jolly Roger. Operating from the Arctic to the Far East, she was the third highest-scoring submarine under the command of Lieut.-Commander H.A.V. Haggard. BELOW: the dial-filled interior of Tradewind.

room. We certainly got a lively reception. A few minutes after that a 600-ton schooner came on the scene and the captain was going to have a go at that with the gun but when he asked the other officers' opinions they disagreed so we crept off to a safe area in case destroyers came out looking for us. This captain is certainly mad, taking stupid risks. We will be lucky to get back to port again if he carries on this way. Hope we get our own captain back when we reach port, if we do.

July 15. A quiet day, thank goodness. The invasion of Sicily is going according to plan.

July 16. Went to gun action stations when we saw a 1,000-ton patrol vessel of some sort. Captain had a look and remarked "It's only got one gun aft." We got closer and he saw it also had one forward and two midships. We all groaned, expecting a hot reception from those guns if we surfaced and went gunning this ship. An Italian bomber came on the scene, then flew right low over us just as the captain was looking through the periscope. The water was flat calm and our whole outline was visible even at 60 feet. We flooded our quick-diving tank to get us out of the way of the expected bombs. Then the explosions came, near, but we were well on our way down. We levelled off at 350 feet and went back to normal routine. Kept down for an hour. We came back to periscope depth and the ship was out of sight. In the afternoon we received a signal telling us to move to another billet. With three other submarines we are to patrol in a line across the Gulf of Taranto. We are about 140 miles from here and we have to be on billet by 0400 tomorrow morning. The captain decided to surface two hours before sunset. Imagine, steaming along in full daylight in the Adriatic with enemy territory all around you!

Taranto is the largest naval port in Italy and we presume we are there to stop any ships leaving to help the fight against us in our invasion of Sicily. Also if they evacuate Sicily, we can catch them coming over, so our job seems important.

July 18. Nothing came through yet. We are all hoping to see some big stuff try to get past us. We have 14 torpedoes left so can do a power of damage.

July 20. This morning at about 0300 a dark object was seen far ahead of us so we began to chase it on the surface. She was zigzagging wildly all over the place but we got six torpedoes ready to fire when an enemy destroyer came on the scene so we had to dive out of her way. We went into silent routine and managed to get away after an hour of depth-charging.

July 21. Still no sign of enemy ships entering or leaving the harbour. Being too near Sicily it may have been put out of action by the Italians.

July 22. About 0100 this morning the lookouts on the bridge saw a plane pass right in front of us and a flare was dropped. We thought it may be a pilot baling out so we raced to the spot, only to find a flare burning on the water. We immediately guessed it was a signal for some enemy ship giving away our position, so we turned tail and went as fast as possible away from the spot.

About 0300 a ship was spotted right behind us, the moon came up then and it was found to be an enemy submarine. She was just getting ready to fire torpedoes at us so we crash dived just in time. Our asdic operator heard one whizz over our heads as we got below the surface. It exploded in the distance at the end of its run. We heard three more explosions, a near thing. We got our torpedoes ready to attack her. Up periscope and we were just in time to see her diving only a mile away. My place of duty is in the control room, on the panel, so the officer of the watch and myself kept constant periscope watch alternately just in case she surfaced again. No luck, she kept down.

July 23. Another quiet day. We are probably patrolling near the shore. In fact we went in to two miles from it and took photographs through the periscope of the vast anti-invasion defences all up the coast, in the toe of Italy. Barbed wire entanglements, anti-tank measures and simply littered with pill boxes. They are certainly scared of a big invasion.

July 24. Still nothing happening yet. We have got our recall and we leave the billet on the 26th for Beirut.

I left *Trooper* sick. She then went out on patrol again and was sunk. They say she hit a mine but we shall never know exactly what happened. It has shaken me up terribly. If I hadn't been taken ill I would be food for the fishes by this time so I consider myself very lucky.

When you think of the patrols you have done on the boat and the happy times under difficult conditions, cheery talk while getting depth-charged, all those details live in your memory and to think that they will never speak again, never return to port again. But it is the fortunes of war that I missed her and so am alive to go back to my darling again.

The submarine is gone but she and her crew will forever live in my memory.

Because of the shortage of torpedo targets in the Indian Ocean and South China Sea from 1944 onwards, British submarines were loaded with additional gun ammunition. Here four-inch shells are being stowed in the lower torpedo racks, converted for the purpose in H.M.S. Trump in 1945.

It wasn't Cricket

He could have killed us

by Alf Gower

Seawolf had just left Dundee in 1941 after undergoing a refit. The crew had consumed their share of duty-free beer (4d. a pint), it was a beautifully sunny day and we felt relaxed. I was on the bridge with Smokey, our leading signalman.

We proceeded port side of a convoy when a Blenheim appeared and started to fly fore and aft to us and the convoy and we felt sheltered. We had not carried out trim dive – indeed, it would have been dangerous to do so in such a busy estuary.

The pilot of the Blenheim waved to us and our navigating officer, who was duty officer, waved back. The Blenheim flew nearer and its pilot waved again and, yet again, our navvy returned the wave. The plane flew still nearer and again the pilot waved. Our navvy said: "What's the matter with this . . .?" and halfway between his returning wave, he screamed: "Dive, Dive, Dive." He had noticed that on turning the Blenheim, although having British markings below the plane had a German swastika above. "Blaa, Blaa, Blaa" went the harsh tones of the klaxon. Smokey and I scrambled down the hatch, reaching the control room arms and legs entwined in each other's. We disengaged and I ran to my diving station in the fore-ends but just as I passed the wardroom, the wardroom flunkey, Darby Allen, said: "Don't panic, Alf, it's only a trim dive." I shouted: "Is it, well you listen to this!" The bomb fell, our fore hatch lifted of its seating, water poured into the boat until the hatch sprang back again and the boat shook and shivered. What a way to be nearly bowled out on a beautifully sunny day.

Undine

by A.B. Percy Campbell

I was recalled to the Submarine Service just prior to the outbreak of hostilities in 1939 and was drafted to L27, a submarine of some vintage, built after World War I and due for the scrapyard. However I was quite happy, as I was familiar with the "L" class boats and it didn't take long to settle in. We were attached to the 6th Flotilla and operated from Blyth. We were commanded by Captain (S) Jock Bethell, who had served in submarines in the Great War as a young lieutenant and had in consequence great experience, having served most of his life in subs.

Blyth became untenable as a submarine base due to the Tyne and Blyth being mined by German aircraft using magnetic mines, so the whole 6th Flotilla moved to Rosyth. It was from here that I sailed on my first war patrol in L27. Our billet was off Bergen and our job was to seek out the enemy and engage him. We were dived during the hours of daylight, at periscope depth, which in L boats meant 30 feet, and surfaced at night to charge our batteries. While on the surface only three people manned the bridge; the officer of the watch and two lookouts, one to port and one to starboard. The watch was of two hours' duration and that was more than enough, as scanning the horizon through binoculars in pitch darkness was very trying. After a while you imagine you see lights that don't exist. However everything must be reported and the bearing given. Nothing was left to chance.

Our patrol was uneventful and we made our way back to base. At about 30 miles off the coast we received our first taste of war. We were on the surface doing 11 knots when suddenly the diving klaxon sounded and we crash dived. Before we were completely submerged we heard gurgling noises and a loud plop. We were being attacked by three of our own aircraft who were rather bomb-happy, had mistaken us for an enemy U-boat and didn't wait to ask questions. We in our turn did not wait to fire the recognition signal.

"Flood bow buoyancy," ordered the captain, "100 feet."

The boat took on a steep angle, the bow went to 180 feet, and the fore-endsmen began to sweat. We all knew that L boats in the autumn of their lives were limited to a maximum of 80 feet as their pressure hulls were getting rather thin.

"Blow Nos. 1 and 2 main ballast," came the order.

This done the lovely old lady responded and levelled off at 100 feet. She did, however, take in a bit of water which gave us no little concern.

The aircraft up above continued their attack and scared the hell out of us. It's an uncanny feeling to hear the plop and gurgling sound as the bombs or charges they were dropping passed us by, missing their target by several yards. We blessed the bomb aimers for their inefficiency. The captain behaved magnificently during this period and in about half an hour ordered the cox'n to bring her up to periscope depth.

"Up periscope." "Surface."

The captain made his way up the conning tower, followed by the signalman, opened the hatch and in a joking voice said to the signalman: "That was a near one, Bunts, we will have to have a nice talk to the R.A.F. boys."

"Course 270, 220 revs."

The engines grunted a little and in a couple of hours or so we were alongside the parent ship at Rosyth. We learned afterwards that the R.A.F. had bombed us, and had they used depth charges we would have had it.

L27 was taken off offensive patrols and was relegated to training at Fort Blockhouse. I was drafted to *Undine,* a small but modern boat of 550 tons. The crew numbered 27 officers and men and she was built for coastal patrol – but they didn't say which coast. This class were very small boats but they carried a very good armament, six 21-inch torpedo tubes and a three-inch gun. They were ugly-looking ducklings with a large bulging bow which enclosed two torpedo tubes outside the pressure hull. They were single hull boats and gave you a rough time at sea, but what we liked most of all was that she could dive in 25 seconds, which was very fast compared to the large types of boat. That gave some measure of comfort.

Living conditions didn't exist. The seamen and stokers had four bunks between them, chiefs and P.O.s had four and the officers four. When off watch we slept and ate where we could. Washing was out of order and we were lucky to have a cup of water to clean our teeth. If one's mouth felt clean, it didn't matter about the other parts of one's anatomy. From the time we left harbour on patrol until we returned, we didn't undress. We wore overalls over our heavy white woollen frocks, long pants and sea boots. All our kit was left aboard the parent ship. We grew beards, perhaps to hide our dirty faces, and vied with each other to see who could grow the best. Our captain, Lieut-Commander Jackson, grew a splendid Capt. Cuttle type of beard. Had there been a real competition he would have won.

Life in submarines during the war was pretty tough. Everyone knew his job thoroughly and indeed knew every other man's job. There was more self discipline rather than the rigid discipline which was customary in other services, and this was appreciated. We were very proud to serve in what was called "The Trade."

In the first year of the war things were very hard on submarine crews as every available one was at sea on patrol. On return to harbour after three weeks and feeling pretty worn out, half the crew were given a few days' leave while the other half set to to unload the torpedoes. This in itself was a tremendous task, and then we took on a fresh supply, cleaned up the boat and reprovisioned her, etc. There was no spare crew to carry out these arduous tasks or for preparing the boat for sea again. Everything was done by the crew themselves. Things did improve in time, when those at the top of the tree realised that human beings can take only so much and crews returning from sea should be rested.

Such was the state of affairs when on December 31, 1939, *Undine* left base at Blyth on what was to be her last patrol. The harbours around Blyth were receiving a lot of attention from the Luftwaffe, who were sowing their magnetic mines, which made us a little unhappy and we were always on tenterhooks until we were well out into the North Sea, when we all felt much safer. We left at 1600, preceded by a small minesweeper, continued on the surface at 12 knots and dived at dawn. The captain then announced our area of operations and what we were expected to accomplish.

"Seek out and engage enemy warships and investigate, plot and chart the swept channel in the minefields off Heligoland."

We had strict orders not to sink unarmed merchant ships. At this time we were fighting the war with kid gloves on. Enemy warships were few and far between but our enthusiasm was whetted by our sister ship *Ursula,* whose captain, Lieut-Commander Phillips, sank a Koln class cruiser a couple of weeks previously. On that same patrol the pride of the German merchant fleet, the Hamburg America liner *Bremen,* passed his sights within 800 yards – a beautiful target, but observing the Geneva Convention he could not press home his attack and had to let her pass. Those aboard the *Bremen* didn't know how lucky they were.

On January 7, 1940, *Undine* was at watch diving stations at periscope depth, speed about three knots, heading slowly and cautiously towards Heligoland. The sea was very calm, indeed flat as a millpond, and consequently the captain was very careful in using the periscope. I was at the foreplanes at the time and concentrating on keeping the boat at precisely 28 feet to enable the periscope to be used to the best advantage, with only a foot or so protruding above the surface, when there was a loud explosion which made the large depth gauge in front of me vibrate somewhat. An alteration of course was made a few degrees to starboard and the captain ordered "Up periscope." He carefully conned the 360 degrees, in the course of which he spotted what he thought looked like a marker buoy. He called Lieut. Senior, the navigator, to have a look and came to the conclusion it could be a marker for the swept channel he had hoped to find. Several other explosions occurred without causing any serious damage but it was agreed that we were in a minefield. We learned afterwards that they were controlled mines operated from a shore base in Heligoland. In other words the enemy knew we were there but we did not realize this at the time.

Several alterations of course were made and eventually we were clear and we were thankful for the reprieve. In about an hour our silence was disturbed by the sound of the klaxon's "diving stations." I was relieved by the second coxswain, who took over the foreplanes and went forward to the torpedo room. The order "Bring Nos. 1 and 2 tubes to the ready, blow WRT, open 1 and 2 bow caps" came from the captain, followed in quick succession by the gyro angle, which was immediately set on Nos. 1 and 2 torpedoes and we reported them ready back to the control room. The captain had spotted three ships which seemed to be a cross between destroyers and ocean-going trawlers. They were, on closer observation, hunting craft, two in line ahead and the other bearing in on the starboard bow.

Red Cross parcels provide welcome winter relief for ratings from Undine, who were temporarily held at Oflag IXA prisoner-of-war camp for officers at the beginning of 1940. Able Seaman P. Campbell is in the centre of the trio.

After firing the two torpedoes we went as deep as we could, which was only 80 feet, and scraped along the bottom. It was a pity we didn't have deeper water in which to manoeuvre. We waited silently and counted the seconds waiting for our torpedoes to hit. We counted 40, 41, 42, 43, etc. – they should have hit by now. Everyone was tense with excitement and then there was a tremendous explosion, the like of which we have never experienced before. Our kipper had got home, or so we thought,and then three more loud explosions followed in quick succession which shook *Undine* and smashed a few lights.

"Close all watertight doors, rig for depth charging," snapped the captain.

We lay on the bottom and silently waited for the next pattern. The enemy ships had seen the wake of our torpedoes as the sea was dead calm, and taken evasive action. Our torpedoes had missed by three metres, so we were to learn afterwards. It was easy meat for them as they only had to set their depth charges to 80 feet and it was only a matter of time before our number was up. We could hear them criss-crossing at full speed over the top of us and just waited for the next blow to come – and come it did. It scared the hell out of us as it was a near direct hit.

The coupling on the main air line in the torpedo room sprang, making a deafening screaming noise as air at 3,000 p.s.i. released itself into the fore-ends. Suddenly the bow lifted and shot to the surface. The drop keel had been dislodged by the last explosion, giving the boat six tons of positive buoyancy. We were now at their mercy. The forepoart, from the bows to the conning tower, was on the surface, and the afterpart still submerged. We tried every possible means to get her down, when they opened fire with their three-inch gun and machine-gunned us as fast as they could. We could hear hits on the pressure hull hull.

"Abandon ship, every man for himself – sorry, chaps," said the captain.

Lieut. Sam Stewart, our youngest officer, was calmly setting fire to our code books and the confidential papers in the wardroom. I went to his assistance to give him a hand and he told me with a smile on his face to open up battery ventilation inboard and with the mainline seacocks fully open, we made our exit. The Germans ceased fire when they saw us in the water and lowered two seaboats and picked us up. The water was extremely cold and we couldn't have been in very long although it seemed ages. After ten minutes, or it may have been less, while we were prisoners aboard the German ship, we heard an explosion and the Germans informed us that *Undine* had blown up with five of their crew on board. They, in their efforts to keep her afloat and take her as a prize, were thwarted by the efforts of Sam Stewart, the smiling one.

From Heligoland we were taken to Wilhelmshaven, interrogated and detained there for ten days before being transferred to a prisoner-of-war camp. While we were at Wilhelmshaven we met the survivors of *Starfish,* another of the 6th Flotilla from Blyth who two days after, met the same fate as *Undine.* Another sub, *Seahorse,* from our group and operating in the same area, failed to return to base and was lost with all hands. Presumably she struck a mine and vanished as the Germans had no knowledge of her. In one week the 6th Flotilla had been reduced to half its number. It must have been a terrible blow to Jock Bethell, captain (S) of the Flotilla, and in consequence of his protestations to the Lords of the Admiralty, our submarines were withdrawn from operating on "Hitler's cabbage patch" as Winston preferred to call it.

So ended my fighting career as a submariner and for the next five-and-a-half years I was to rot in prisoner-of-war camps. On reflection, I think those of us who survived serving in submarines during the war were very lucky, as we were informed that our losses were 78 per cent. But I suppose we were comforted to know that the German submarine losses were a great deal more.

The Deep Dive

by J. R. Creswell

'Twas a cold day in Inchmarnock,
The coldest day of the year,
And the crew of the submarine Strongbow
Were silent and shaking with fear.

They had left the Forth in the forenoon
With many a jest and a crack.
They had all written home the night before
For they weren't sure they'd come back.

The purpose of their trip that day
Was to thoroughly test out the hull.
The captain intended to take her deep,
And our cup of woe was full.

The crew had gone to their stations
And the klaxon blared through the boat.
A lookout fell down the conning tower,
And tore the back off his coat.

The captain gave the depth required,
Slowly we slipped out of sight.
For once we had perfect trim,
And everything seemed quite all right.

Swiftly we fell through the water,
The gauge read three forty feet,
The whole boat started to quiver,
And I nearly fell off my seat.

With a crash we hit the bottom,
The asdics transmitted K's,
The fore-ends crew left their stations
And stood by their D.S.E.A.s.

The WT Office went all adrift,
And so did the HSD,
He reported the signals as being K's
When Sardonyx was sending out C.

The chef was reading the Wizard,
He casually glanced at the gauge,
And keeping an eye on his tanksides,
He started to read the next page.

A stoker fell down the pump room,
His nerves had turned to pulp.
He quickly pulled out his bottle
And drank it all at a gulp.

The captain sprang into action –
He ordered "Blow One's, Three's and Five's"
And the rest of the crew, while the E.R.A. blew,
Were wishing they'd led better lives.

Swiftly we rose to the surface
We knew it had been a close call,
And we explained it to the "Bunting",
Who had slept right through it all.

Una

Of the many submarine gun actions which took place during World War Two, one which could qualify as the strangest happened aboard H.M.Submarine *Una.* Patrolling from Malta during 1942-3, she sighted an Italian schooner running close inshore, probably near Tripoli. As these craft were often employed in stores and ammunition running, they were a fair target. Gun action was ordered, *Una* surfaced and closed the schooner. To encourage the Italian crew to abandon ship without bloodshed, the Lewis gun was mounted on the bridge and a few bursts went through the rigging. There appeared to be some reluctance on the part of the Italians, therefore it became necessary to engage them with the main armament, i.e. the 12-pounder deck gun.

The gun, believe it or not, bore the breech crest of VR, and had orignally been a field gun used in the Boer War. Unlike the fixed ammo used in later U-class submarines, these guns had separate projectile and charge. The magazine, just forward of the control room, also doubled as a food store, and it was here that the ammo was kept in canvas holders ready for hoisting up to the bridge, where the loading number – usually the "Bunting Tosser" – fed the ammo down a drop stop loading chute to the gun. Some of the spare canvas ammo carriages were used by the "tanky" and the coxswain to apportion soups, meats and juices for the daily menus, ready to hand to the chef to perform his culinary artistry. A canvas carrier full of beans, herring and tins of vegetable soup would probably weigh as much as two "proggies" and two charges. Such was the noise during the action and the frantic hauling up and down of the chute that it was not possible to warn the gun's crew they may have loaded a bin of "Fifty-seven varieties," followed by cordite charge. When the beans burst above the schooner's deck, its crew very promptly decided to hop over the side as they were being attacked by a boatful of mad Englishmen.

To make fair comment on this action the beans could have been Crosse and Blackwell's, but they were certainly not Harris's Famous Tinned Bacon, which came in a flat tin.

In a later gun action, *Una,* with her C.O., Lieut.-Commander Martin, R.N., chased another schooner into a tiny coastal village and surfaced in broad daylight. As the gun's crew manned and engaged the target, there suddenly appeared from behind the little white-washed houses down by the beach what appeared to be a mobile 88mm. gun or possibly a tank, which engaged *Una* with some very accurate shooting. *Una* was hit several times in her bridgeworks but in spite of there being several people on the bridge, no one was hit. It was obviously prudent to break off the engagement, the bridge was cleared and the gun's crew ordered below. *Una* turned away to steer an opposite course, and as the last of the gun's crew was "cocking his dish" to climb over the bridge coaming, he announced that he had been "shot up the arse," to which those present agreed "Haven't we all?"

Diving with great difficulty and bouncing on a shallow bottom, *Una* eventually submerged out of range and was fortunate to have suffered no hit on the pressure hull. The gun's crew member, who rejoiced in the nickname of "Panda" due to his dark, woolly bear appearance, had in fact been hit exactly where he said he had been, but being inclined to moderate corpulence, had sufficient flesh to absorb the shrapnel splinters. *Una* returned to Lazaretto Creek, landed the Panda and resumed her patrol. The Panda, after a spell of treatment and recuperation, rejoined *Una* and completed the commission, returning to the UK about March, 1943.

H42 (Memoriam)

by A. Bidmead, H.M.S. Walker

To the Glory of God, there lies asleep,
Beneath the Mediterranean-deep,
The stalwart hearts of a stalwart crew,
Who gave their lives in H42.

No hand of man could save the shock
That sunk her off Gibraltar Rock;
No hand but God's could stay the wave,
That claimed them to its watery grave.

A moment only and all was o'er,
They died in harness as in war;
A glorious death, a glorious cause,
May all who read this make a pause,
To pray for those who fought for you
And gave their all in H42.

Kippers

by Alf Gower, Norwich branch, S.O.C.A.

On the *Seawolf* when "Crash" Cook was the coxswain, we were known as "Crash Cook and his Forty Thieves." We arrived from patrol to Holy Loch and tied up alongside *Forth.* I was on deck watch when the boys told me there was a box of Gordon's gin on *Forth's* foc'sle, so we decided to have it and a hurried relief was found for me. Up we went to the foc'sle and, surrounded by the other ratings, I carried the box down to the mess deck. We were going to have a grand old p--- up.

The box was addressed to my old friend, Admiral Bonham Carter (in Chatham, 1940, previous to joining boats, he weighed me off with 30 stoppages of pay and leave, 14 days' No. 11, and three months' second class for leave). It had been sent by Admiral Little, so coming from an admiral it should taste nice. When we got to the messdeck and opened it up, lo and behold, it held nothing else but kippers, layer upon layer of them. Presumably they were being sent from one admiral to the wardroom of another.

We were dumbfounded. For a change I was at a loss what to do until I hit on the idea of approaching Crash. I asked him what we were having for breakfast the following morning. He said "Bacon and red lead," asked me why, and I replied that he could have some kippers if he wanted them. He exploded.

"Take those .... things away – there are signals going out all over the fleet about them."

I said: "Well, what can I do with them?"

"Throw them over the b----- side," said Crash.

Being the green kid that I was, I did just that. The next morning I didn't feel so clever with all those kippers floating around the boat. I was thoroughly embarrassed.

Tactician in the Far East

by W. A. Horton

Way back in 1944, the "Super T" *Tactician* set off from Trinco (Trincomalee in Ceylon). A week's trip on the surface to our patrol line before diving. A strange cargo, two folded kayaks, rubber dinghies, cans of petrol, cases of provisions and a couple of passengers, not submariners. Aye! a cloak and dagger job, no doubt to one of the many uninhabited islands where lookout wireless posts were being set up or already operating, passing back information of shipping movements. Japs, of course.

Surfacing, we arrived seemingly at dusk. We crept towards this island under the Jimmy's eye. My fellow upper deckhand and I assembled the two kayaks in the very limited space of the fore ends, more like a cargo hold. The forehatch was opened, up went the kayaks, over the side, made fast to the lower jumping wire. The rubber dinghies were next. Our passengers soon pumped them up and over the side they went. We looked like the boating part of the Serpentine. Then to work for some hours – not many, for darkness was a short duration – and supplies were ferried ashore. After the first trip, two strangers appeared. They were whisked off to the wardroom (for big eats, I was told later) and it seemed they were being relieved by our two passengers.

On the order from the skipper on the bridge to secure, the rubber dinghies were deflated and the kayaks passed below. The fore hatch was shut, the second cox'n passing below to secure. On climbing the bridge from the casing, the skipper asked my colleague and I if we would like a swim as he could see we were soaked in perspiration. Over the side we went – it was super. When we returned to the bridge, dripping sea water, the First Lieutenant said: "Well done, now shake the chief stoker, ask him to put air on the fresh water line and you can each have one bowl of water to rinse off the salt." The chief had a right drip on, but when we told him what we had been doing he relented.

We dived and shoved off to our patrol line at 0400. That evening, around 2230, we surfaced, returning to the island while it was still light. Over the tannoy came, to our astonishment: "Hands to bathe in five minutes' time, open gun tower hatches, upper and lower."

So all bar those actually on watch went over the side. I can see the skipper now, slipping his "sarong" off and plunging off the bow. Once again on board we carried on as the night before! Kayaks, rubber dinghies, loading and sending supplies ashore. The first returning kayaks brought two more strangers, who were soon installed in the wardroom. We completed the job that night but there was no more swimming and we dived at dawn to resume patrol.

I heard from the wardroom steward later that the second pair of

Proudly sporting their Jolly Roger, complete with cloak-and-dagger mission symbols, the crew of Tactician line the casing.

passengers reported to the skipper that a Jap destroyer had been patrolling round the island during the afternoon. I wonder what the Jap Emperor would have thought had he known that a British submarine had used his waters for a boating lake and swimming pool. I also wonder if the skipper entered the "Hands to bathe" in his log for the Captain (S) to see.

Unbending

Recollections of G.H. Douglas

It is more than 40 years ago now and time has dimmed my memory. In fact I can barely remember certain patrols, but others are still fairly clear and I will try to recall them as faithfully as possible. Not having access to any official records, however, there may be places and dates not exactly correct, but I will be as accurate as I can and relate events as I saw them from a lower deck point of view – and some of which are certainly not in any official history.

I joined *Unbending,* or P37 as she was then, as an A.B. S/T at the submarine base H.M.S. Ambrose in Dundee in June, 1942, with another A.B. named Bill Ball, who lived in Preston, Lancs. We joined on a Saturday morning, having travelled overnight from Fort Blockhouse, and sailed from the U.K. for Gibraltar on the Monday afternoon. Dundee and the submarine base at Blyth were the two most popular bases in the U.K. for one very simple reason – duty-free beer at sixpence a pint (pre-decimal currency). Being a light drinker, this had no special attraction for me but it rated very highly with the majority of ratings.

Unbending had then been in commission for about six months and her crew were highly trained. My first recollection was the number of stroppy crew members, undoubtedly influenced by the fact that it was my first operational submarine. Before the weekend had elapsed, one crew member was on the Captain's report – I think the charge was disobedience of a direct order. He subsequently left the boat in Gibraltar after a further charge and I was one of the escort detailed to take him to detention quarters on the Rock. After we had delivered him, the gate crashed and we heard orders being screamed at him to double away. We all thought: "Better you than me, Jack."

At noon on Monday, shortly before we were due to sail from Dundee, almost half of the seamen and stokers were in a public house a short distance from the quayside and the coxswain had to be dispatched to order the crew out. The order was obeyed with some reluctance on the part of one or two, and half an hour later we had slipped and were en route to Gibraltar. *Unbending* was under the command of Lieut. Winter and we proceeded on the surface most of the way, only diving for part of the crossing of the Bay of Biscay. After an uneventful voyage, we duly tied up alongside *H.M.S. Maidstone,* the depot ship at Gibraltar.

The next few days were spent painting ship, re-storing and routine maintenance, after which we proceeded on a 48-hour shakedown patrol. It was during this that a most unfortunate incident occurred. We were on the surface at night, just off Malaga, and had sighted a Spanish or neutral merchant ship, when the order came from the bridge.

"For exercise, hands to gun action stations."

The crew doubled to their stations and I was in the tube space with the T.I. and the other fore-endsmen, A.B.s Johnny Downs, a Londoner, and Joe Edmonds, from Nottingham. After about ten minutes the order "Blow up Nos. One and Two tubes" was received in the tube space. This created some uncertainty because the vital words "For exercise" were not included in the order and we knew that we were still at gun action stations.

At this point the torpedo officer arrived in the tube space and on his confirmation of the order, it was carried out. Seconds later the indicator flashed to "Fire" and away went two torpedoes. Miraculously the merchant ship was not hit but some two or three minutes later there was a resounding explosion from the direction of the Spanish coast. Astonishingly, no one at this time, except those in the tube space, were aware that torpedoes had been fired, because we were on the surface and the night was dark. The T.I. was now called to the control room to look at the gyro compass, which had come off the board, whether or not as a result of the explosion I'm not sure. He remarked to the First Lieutenant that only one of the torpedoes had exploded. The First Lieutenant was somewhat shocked by the report and it was with some trepidation that the news was conveyed to the bridge. We duly returned to *Maidstone* minus two torpedoes, to the inevitable investigation. Subsequently, Lieut. E. Stanley took over command of *Unbending*.

The investigation delayed our departure for Malta for some time and the delay was further lengthened by another mishap. Our batteries had to be removed for a reason unknown to me, although I believe it was routine for all boats. It was a back-breaking task, working in shifts day and night, manhandling the cells, which weighed several hundredweight each, out of the boat and on to the jetty. It had, of course, all to be done over again putting them back, and during this operation one or more of the cells was connected up in reverse, with resulting loss of capacity and charging difficulties. Three or four weeks elapsed before the trouble was located and rectified. One result of our delay was several changes in the ship's company, and we finally sailed for Malta in September, 1942, with a number of new faces on board.

Malta was then still under siege conditions but nothing like the earlier months of the war, and the heavy air attacks were virtually over. There were still shortages, however, and the naval strength was the newly-formed 10th Flotilla based at Manoel Island, the MTB Flotilla, and a couple of minesweepers. It was the 10th Flotilla under Captain Simpson which we joined in October. I remember entering Lazaretto Creek for the first time and can still see the church at the entrance to the creek with a huge hole in the steeple. We later learned that it was caused by a shell from one of our anti-aircraft guns positioned on Manoel Island.

There was no delay here. We had a talk from Captain Simpson, who explained the situation in Malta, a couple of days storing ship, a fresh coat of dark blue paint and we were off on our first patrol. We were escorted out of harbour by a minesweeper, then we were on our own. A trim dive, and then on to our first billet off the North African coast.

Within a day or two we had made our first sinking. It was a surface night attack on a small tanker, unescorted and attempting to slip through in the darkness with supplies for the German Army. It was due to the sharpness and efficiency of our lookouts that it was detected, as our U-class submarines at that time were not fitted with radar. We fired a salvo and scored at least one hit on the target, with devastating results. The tanker, which must have been loaded with aviation spirit, virtually disintegrated, and the bridge personnel reported blazing debris scattered over a wide area.

The following day, or perhaps a day later, we carried out a gun action against a small coaster, again unescorted. Unlike the later U-class, which carried a three-inch gun, *Unbending* was armed with a 12-pounder only and although we almost exhausted our supply of ammunition, the coaster was still afloat and it was necessary to board her and finish her off with an explosive charge, sustaining a bent bow in the process.

Two sinkings in as many days and no counter-attacks – the crew were now highly elated. The third attack, however, was to prove different. This was against an Italian convoy of four merchant ships, heavily escorted by six destroyers, and we attacked from very close range with a full salvo. Our torpedoes were set at a depth of 12 feet although I remember the depth mechanism on one tube would not engage and the setting had to remain at eight feet. We scored hits on a merchant ship of some 5,000 tons and one of the escorting destroyers, both later confirmed as sunk. The remaining destroyers counter-attacked and about 60 depth charges were dropped, but Lieut. Stanley cleverly dived under the convoy and the charges were not close enough to do any damage.

The convoy and escort re-formed and some time later came under further attacks from *Unbroken* under the command of Lieut. Mars. This was unsuccessful and *Unbroken* was heavily counter-attacked and suffered severe damage to her batteries, necessitating her return to the dockyard in Grand Harbour with her crew in gas masks for protection from chlorine gas. *Unbending* sank another small ship on this patrol in a gun action and returned to Manoel Island in triumph with five sinkings to her credit. This was our most successful patrol. None of the others produced as many targets, which by now were not so plentiful as earlier in the war.

I remember one in the early months of 1943. We were on patrol in the Straits of Messina, the stretch of water between Sicily and Italy, and a large merchant ship was sighted under tow by a couple of tugs and escorted by a destroyer. Lieut. Stanley manoeuvred into a firing position and carried out the attack with four torpedoes. Immediately after firing we turned, grouped up on the motors and put as much distance as possible between us and the point of attack before we were located by the escort.

All the time we were waiting and listening, and after about twc minutes we heard two loud explosions. A few minutes later, we clearly heard the cracking and breaking-up sounds indicating another sinking, followed by the sound of propellers overhead. The destroyer was hunting us. We were heavily counter-attacked for the next two or three hours, counting some 80 or 90 depth charges, some close enough to affect our trim with some frightening angles and minor interior damage but nothing serious. The destroyer eventually lost contact and we could resume patrol. We came up to periscope depth and the captain ordered: "Up periscope" but nothing happened. It was well and truly jammed. There was no alternative – we made a signal and set course for Malta. We sailed through the night with the E.R.A.s working on the periscope and after three or four hours they succeeded in freeing it, and we altered course to resume our patrol. It was a brief return, however, and we were soon recalled to base.

Much has been written about the efficiency and bravery (or lack of it) of the Italians, but in my experience this was not so. On one patrol in particular we sighted an Italian destroyer and before we could close up to diving stations we had been detected, either by asdic or their lookouts had spotted our periscope. We dived deeper and the destroyer dropped three patterns of nine depth charges each. They were fairly close but we suffered no damage. We were now prepared for the worst but for some unaccountable reason they broke off the attack, leaving us to resume patrol somewhat shaken.

On another occasion we went to gun action stations with a small minesweeper. We had all the advantages of surprise and were able to get off several rounds before they were aware of us. Our fire was not accurate enough and the Italian captain was not overawed. They opened up with a heavy machine-gun but fortunately they, too, were not accurate or our gun's crew would all have been casualties. We were compelled to crash dive. About fifteen to twenty seconds was all it took for a U-class to reach periscope depth and minutes later we heard the familiar propeller sounds. About a dozen depth charges were dropped, which luckily must have been all they carried, but none was close enough to do any damage. That was one Italian who earned our respect. One of the other boats in the flotilla – I believe it was *United* – had one of her gun crew killed during a similar attack.

Not all patrols involved torpedo attacks and gun actions. We had a few special operations, usually landing commando units behind enemy lines. I remember the first, when we took on board two Army commandos, one of whom was a heavily built, tough-looking private. On one occasion he went down into the Auxiliary Machine Space and the hatch slipped, striking him on the head. A normal person would have been knocked unconscious but he simply shook his head and carried on. We landed them behind the German lines in North Africa and I often wonder if he was as tough with the enemy. We never found out, as they did not return to the rendezvous and I can only assume they were killed or captured.

On another occasion, we landed four or five commandos in Italy. They, too, were extremely tough and fit-looking and armed with a formidable arsenal of weapons, but again they failed to return to the rendezvous. After this operation, we carried on with our patrol and sighted a medium-sized merchant ship, which was unescorted and must have obscured our periscope, because she tried to escape by running into a narrow inlet. We pursued her and eventually she ran aground. We made one hit on her with a torpedo but could only claim a hit, not a sinking.

After the pursuit we, too, managed to run aground although we were still partially submerged, and were held fast for several minutes. During this time someone ashore opened up with a machine gun, the bullets hammering against the pressure hull below the surface. After stopping and starting the motors with all the power we had, we eventually broke free and proceeded astern into deeper water, where it was wide enough to turn round and head out to sea, very thankful that nothing heavier than a machine gun was used against us when we were so helpless.

During our return to Malta from this patrol, we received a signal that one of our aircraft had been shot down in our area and we were to look for survivors, thought to be in a rubber dinghy. We had their estimated position but as it was a dark night and us being low in the water, it would be like looking for a needle in a haystack to sight so small an object. The miracle happened and we sighted it, a small yellow rubber dinghy with one R.A.F. sergeant in it – the only survivor. We pulled him aboard, with his dinghy, which was deflated and stored in the fore-ends, and he appeared to be in pretty good shape despite his ordeal. He was extremely thankful, to say the least, and but for the skill of our navigator and the sharp eyes and efficiency of our lookouts, he would undoubtedly have been picked up in daylight by the Italians and finished the war as a prisoner. So on that patrol, we left Malta with the Army and returned with the R.A.F.

Another special operation was a highly secret one, landing special R.N. commando teams to survey suitable beaches in Sicily for the Allied invasion then being planned. The operation was to last for about a week, and all four re-load torpedoes were removed from the boat and their place taken by two long canoes. We reached our billet and every night for about a week, we disembarked the team with their canoes. This was a rather nerve-wracking experience as it entailed opening the fore-ends to unload the unwieldy craft, which were not collapsible, and again on the team's return just before dawn. During the period of darkness, we withdrew from the area to charge our batteries and returned before dawn for the pick-up. Throughout the day we lay on the seabed with all non-essential machinery and lights switched off to conserve power, and all ship's company not on watch resting. With the approach of darkness, we made our way submerged, as near inshore as possible to provide commandos with a short paddle to the beach.

During this patrol we were not allowed to attack any enemy shipping and on our return to base, the crew were ordered to maintain silence and not divulge details of the operation to anyone. The dagger sewn on to our Jolly Roger, denoting a special operation, was topped by a top hat, indicating that the mission was to be kept under our hat.

Conditions ashore in Malta were pretty rough and food rationing still prevailed. I remember our bread ration was three loaves a day for 21 ratings (this was before the days of sliced bread), and I achieved a reputation for cutting a loaf into 21 equal slices – and they just had to be equal. On patrol, food was more plentiful and we usually took fresh bread for about five days. On the last day, the remaining loaves had turned a brilliant shade of green and it was necessary to cut off all the sides before it was edible. After this, the cook attempted to bake our own supplies, but it was not always successful. It was prepared whilst dived, then baked on surfacing, but the constant pressure of air during the preparation prevented it from rising properly, and the final result was usually unsatisfactory.

There was a small NAAFI canteen in the base with minimal stock for sale, but every few weeks supplies became available and were distributed to all personnel, each rating receiving an identical package. I suppose this was the fairest method of distribution possible under the circumstances, but it was not satisfactory because many of the items were unwanted. Beer was virtually non-existent and only local wine was available ashore. Because of the shortage of clothing, rig of the day was not enforced and we were able to go ashore in practically any rig, the most favoured outfit being Army battledress. There were no inspections and provided you were not duty watch, we were able to go ashore and return freely, either by local boatman to Valletta or across the bridge from Manoel Island to Sliema.

Towards the end of 1942 or early 1943, the Admiralty decreed that submarines with numbers only should have names. I understand that this was a personal decision of Winston Churchill, and henceforth we were to be *Unbending* and not as previously P37. It was thought at first that we were to be allowed to decide our own names. One boat actually named herself *Ulysses* and affixed a brass nameplate to proclaim it, but Their Lordships frowned on this and we had to accept their chosen names. A small concession was made in that we were allowed to design our own ship's crests. Predictably, the comedians in the companies dreamed up designs of crossed whips, crossed brooms, etc., but there were a few serious submissions and the one chosen for *Unbending* was designed by one of the E.R.A.s. It pictured a sturdy English oak tree, denoting strength and unbending in any storm, and from the trunk ran 37 roots to depict our original number, P37.

For our last patrol, Lieut. Stanley was rested and Lieut. Andrews was in command. Several boats had been lost while carrying out their last patrol before returning to the U.K., and there was a little apprehension on the part of one or two members of the crew, but all fears proved groundless and the patrol was uneventful. I can remember only one incident. Our billet was off North Africa and Lieut. Andrews made frequent use of the periscope. Several of the crew thought it was up too long and too often, and during one lengthy sweep of the surface there was a terrific explosion which sounded not too far away. There had been nothing sighted or picked up by our asdic, and we could only assume that a gun crew ashore had observed our periscope and opened fire. Needless to say, less use was made of the periscope after that.

I served again under Lieut. Andrews in *Subtle*, when we had some success against the Japanese. I was drafted to *Subtle* in February, 1944, having qualified as L.T.O. It was with some unease that I viewed my new boat, as she was all welded, with no rivets, and this was new territory. She was then in the final stages of completion at Cammell Laird's yard at Birkenhead, with workers swarming all over the boat. After securing digs ashore, the routine was to report to the yard each forenoon and the different departments went their various ways, locating spares in the lay-apart store and when possible familiarising ourselves with the layout of the boat.

Whereas my first impressions of *Unbending's* crew were of the stroppiness, my first impression of *Subtle's* was the youthfulness and lack of experience, even among the P.O.s. Many had been detailed off for boats and were not the volunteers of two or three years previously. We were interviewed by the First Lieutenant and his relief was obvious when the few of us who had previous experience reported this. Of course, there were not enough experienced hands to commission the number of boats being turned out by the builders.

The aforementioned lay-apart store was a very large structure in which each vessel being built had its own section for spare parts, etc. I suspect it was from here that the nameplate from *Thetis* was acquired, exactly how is a mystery, but some of the dockyard mateys would have sold their mothers to lay their hands on a new pair of pusser's boots. Anyhow, acquired it was and secreted aboard *Subtle* until the end of her commission, somewhere in the engine room, I think.

Eventually, all loose ends were tidied up, the chaos subsided, and after a number of sea trials and tests, *Subtle* was duly handed over by Cammell Laird. Then followed the commissioning ceremony, which all the ship's company attended, followed by a reception to which were invited wives of several of the crew, who had taken advantage of being billeted ashore for a few weeks to bring them to Birkenhead.

The next day or two were spent storing supplies, spares and various items, and in April, 1944, we proceeded to Dunoon. We tied up alongside the depot ship *Forth* and the next few weeks were spent exercising at sea and testing all the equipment.
carried out our deep dive, with some apprehension, I may add. We flooded main ballast tanks and gently dived in stages to the required 500 feet. Apart from a slight creaking of the hull, everything was as it should be, with no leaks or valves blown. The builders had done their job well and the welding passed its first test.

On one of the exercises we carried a small party of R.A.F. aircrew for the experience of a day at sea in a submarine. It was a reciprocal arrangement and later, when we were in Trincomalee, some of our crew went for a flight with them. Everything went well and our guests were suitably impressed, especially when we surfaced. We were blowing main ballast and grouping up when a compensating tank in the stern flooded, due to a faulty valve, I believe, and resulted in a 45-degree stern down angle. With the pump going flat out, it seemed an eternity before we surfaced and levelled off, with the crew white-faced and relieved. The R.A.F. in their innocence were all smiles and the only comment was: "I say, old boy, do you always come up like that?" In the motor room, we then realised that the blocks fitted to the deck had proved their worth.

When we reached Trincomalee, our patrols were usually of a month's duration – a week out, two weeks on the billet, and a week back. We had arrived too late for the big targets, and on the first few patrols we sank three small coasters by torpedo and another by gun action. The principal prey consisted of junks manned by native crews and running supplies to the Japanese garrisons in Malaya. These junks were not considered large enough to merit sinking by torpedo or gunfire, and the usual procedure was to board them and sink them with demolition charges. We sank a number of these vessels, and I remember on one occasion the boarding party returned with a sewing machine which was swiftly hidden in the fore-ends. Trust Jack not to miss a trick. They were shortly followed by the crew of the junk, one of whom was gesticulating and jabbering away, and it was assumed he was the owner of the machine. You could not help but feel sorry for him. His boat had been sunk by villainous-looking strangers, they had shanghaied him aboard their own craft, which had then submerged (only for a few hours, but he was not to know that), and his most treasured possession had been nicked. It was just not his day. I don't suppose the Japs gave them much choice about running supplies. There again, we had no option but to sink them.

In the afternoon of May 9, 1945, we sighted a Japanese heavy cruiser with destroyer escort and went to diving stations. While manceuvring into a firing position, Lieut. Andrews missed his attack and we were unable to get into position for a further attempt. The following day we again sighted the same cruiser on an opposite course to that of the previous day, and still with destroyer escort. We succeeded in getting into a firing position and fired a salvo of six torpedoes. We then shut off for depth charging and altered course for evasive action. Two or three minutes later we heard two explosions and were all convinced we had at least two hits, but later reports confirmed that we had indeed missed and the subsequent counter-attack endured with nothing to show for it. A few minutes later we could detect the asdic impulses bouncing back from our hull and then the old familiar sound of propellers overhead, followed shortly by the deafening explosions of the first pattern. They were not too far away and we had the usual light bulbs smashed. I remember the red alarm light cover in the motor room shattering and getting a slight cut on the knee from flying glass.

Further patterns followed with other minor internal damage but still nothing serious. Then came another which was the closest yet. Our stern was forced down to an unpleasant angle and in addition it caused a loud grating and scratching noise from one of the propeller shafts. We were at silent routine, which made the noise appear even louder, and it seemed at the time that the shaft had been compressed, although we later heard that the force of the charge had compressed the hull, which in turn compressed an internal tank or its mounting against the shaft. The hull sprang back into shape but the internal tank remained scraping the shaft. The motor was stopped and the noise ceased, too. All was quiet again. Further charges were dropped but nothing again as near, and after an hour or two they ceased altogether, and the destroyer broke off the attack and withdrew. Our wireless transmitter was also damaged and on surfacing at night, we were unable to make a report. Thus Lieut. Andrews lost his chance of glory despite having two bites at the cherry. Repairs to the W/T were eventually carried out, the shaft appeared to be undamaged, and other damage being slight, the patrol was resumed without further incident. We returned to Trinco towards the end of May. The much maligned welding had successfully stood up to its first real test, and who knows, a riveted boat might have suffered far more damage.

Repairs, including a few days in the floating dry dock, kept us in Trinco for about six or seven weeks before our next patrol. After the normal ten days' leave to the watch ashore, someone in authority, aware that it would be a few weeks before we were off on patrol again, and assuming that we had nothing better to do with our time, dreamed up the brilliant idea of putting the seamen and stokers through the Army assault course. We all fell in on *Woolf's* quarterdeck in boots and gaiters, complete with rifle and bayonet, with a young, obviously newly qualified G.I. from the *Woolf* in charge. He was full of flannel but *Subtle's* ship's company just refused to be impressed, although by the time we returned, he had the last laugh. We landed and proceeded to the assault course, and with the G.I. and sergeants yelling encouragement, we commenced doubling round the various obstacles. It was soon obvious that an operational submarine's crew were not in the best of condition to double about, and some halfway round we reached a trench eight to ten feet deep, into which we were expected to jump. Most of us landed badly and could only limp the rest of the course and eventually back to the *Woolf.* It was straight to the Sick Bay and I, along with several others, suffered badly jarred heels. We spent the next week hobbling about on crutches.

Woolf was anchored at the far end of the very large harbour, and with the long trip by liberty boat and the limited attractions ashore, many of the ship's company were content to wait for the ten days in Colombo or Kandy. I emember one or two of the boys coming back from a run ashore in Trinco. I think they had had their share of the local arrack because they had visited the local dentist and had one of their teeth replaced by a gold one and returned with million dollar smiles. "Good old Jack." The local gold was really very cheap, as were precious stones such as rubies and emeralds, and the buzz was that somewhere ashore were these mines and only a shovel was needed to provide untold wealth. Apart from jewellers' shops, I never saw any of these jewels and had there been any truth in the rumours, I have no doubt someone would have been in business on the mess deck.

Towards the end of July, we set out on what was to be our last patrol. It was a relatively quiet billet off the Nicobar Islands, from where we radioed back to Trinco the weather conditions and other data relating to weather forecasts. We had a meteorologist aboard for the patrol with all his equipment, including a large balloon and a bottle of gas to inflate it. It was believed on board that we had been given this easy patrol because we still had defects from the last one, but whether or not that was the reason I do not know. I somehow doubt it. The patrol was uneventful and we finally returned to Trinco on August 15, 1945.

We heard about the Japanese surrender on the way back and after we had tied up, one or two of us who had been in it since September, 1939, looked at each other and thought it was all over now and we had come through in one piece. For the first night back, the spare crew took over as trot sentries and all boats alongside prepared to celebrate. The rum was flowing freely and each boat had its quota on the bridge, with sirens and hooters blaring and bells ringing. The more rum consumed, the bigger and louder bangs were looked for, including Verey lights, flares, rockets and eventually star shells from the three-inch. No one seemed to mind or interfere. No doubt the wardroom and the P.O.s were celebrating, too, in their own way.

ABOVE: A fine shot of the bridge of Trump as she sails for England in November, 1945.

BELOW: Room for one more? The fore-ends of Unruffled in 1944.

The Epic of the Seal

By E.R.A. Ernest Trueman

Our troubles started on May 4, 1940. Up till then we had experienced a peaceful patrol, operating in the Kattegat as a minelaying submarine.

At 0200 on May 4 we were lying on the surface having charged our depleted batteries, waiting for dawn and diving stations. At 0215 we dived and as we submerged so came a German aircraft, one of its bombs landing uncomfortably close to us. We sustained no damage and received no more "eggs," so the daily round commenced once more.

Between 1000 and 1100 we were in position and laid our full complement of mines, hoping that Gerry would find them when he least expected or desired it. Then it was "About turn" and homeward bound for another load. At 1830 I was on watch in the control room when a flotilla of enemy "E" boats were sighted right ahead of us. The captain decided that our best plan was to stop all machinery, and in total silence, rest on the seabed till the danger had passed. Accordingly the steering motor and all auxiliary pumps, etc., were stopped and *Seal* slowly sank to the bottom.

The time was 1905 and as I was due to be relieved at 1900 my thoughts turned to supper. Owing to the previous action, however, this meal was late, and so was my relief. As these thoughts passed through my mind there was a terrific explosion and everybody wondered what had happened. All ears were anxiously listening for the next one, everybody assuming that we were being depth-charged by the "E" boats. However none came and the hydroplanes could detect no surface craft in the vicinity.

Suddenly there was pandemonium from aft, and the news passed through that we were making water rapidly in the mining compartment right aft. Those on the spot quickly shut this section off but not before a lot of water had found its way into the mess deck and motor room compartments. It was deemed necessary to evacuate these compartments and all watertight doors were closed up to the engine room.

Conjecture now arose as to what had happened and it was finally decided that we had selected the one spot on the ocean bed to sit on a submerged mine. As soon as the explosion was heard we had started to blow our ballast tanks, but this order was countermanded when only two tanks forward had been partially blown. This had given us an alarming angle up by the bow, stern at 110 feet, bow at 50 feet, length of boat 300 feet, an angle of one in five – most uncomfortable. It was then decided to wait for darkness before attempting to surface in case the enemy should still be in the vicinity. For two hours we lay doing nothing and at 2200 diving stations were called. Every effort was made to lighten the boat. The drop keel was released and auxiliary tanks blown, but still we did not move in the desired direction. These actions had taken us the best part of three hours and by 0100 on May 5, things seemed pretty hopeless.

It was decided to investigate the possibility of entering the motor room, so the Engineer Officer and the C.E.R.A. made tests nd finally gave us the O.K. for entering the motor room. The after DSEA door was then tested and firmly shut, the C.E.R.A. working waist deep in water. It appeared that our stern had sunk into soft mud and was holding us down, so as a last resort all hands, except five of us, were ordered to move right forward. Then orders were given to blow all main ballast tanks and to go full ahead on both motors. We did! Would she rise or would she stick? Seconds seemed like years. At last with a shudder and a jerk and a shake she freed herself from the clutches of the mud and slowly the angle came off and she levelled at 60 feet. Here she hung in the balance seeming neither to rise nor to sink. They were anxious moments, as we now had used our last HP air and if she slipped back we were finished. Game to the last, however, *Seal* gradually rose, until at 0145 she had reched the surface. The conning tower hatch was opened and great gulps of air were the order of the day.

Now our position was this. We had our engines in working order but our steering gear, being in the flooded compartment, was useless. Our bows were pointing in the wrong direction, towards Denmark and Gerry, so our only hope was to go astern towards Sweden, which we could see about ten to fifteen miles distant. This, however, was denied us, as our engines finally seized up owing to the fact that our lubricating oil pumps had decided on a sit-down strike. There we were, helpless, and at 0400 we were sighted by a German seaplane who proceeded to give us the works. At about 0500 we surrendered, and the seaplane took off our captain and one petty officer, telling us they would send assistance.

At 0700 a German trawler came alongside, and so we entered our period of Gefangenshaft on May 5, 1940. Five officers and 48 men of *H.M.S. Seal* for whom, as the Germans informed us, "the war was out." So ended the most anxious hours of my life.

Extract from the Exploits of Tuna

As the moments ticked past and still no counter-attack seemed to be developing, the half-hour passed by, then the hour, and the tension inside the boat seemed to relax as we slowly went dead slow on one motor and began to creep away from what could have been a very unhealthy spot. As the captain stood by me I said: "Excuse me, sir, why is it we haven't been depth-charged?" It seemed so strange to me.

"Well, Roberts, if you were the captain of a U-boat in company with two others and all of a sudden you saw one go up in a cloud of smoke and flame, what would you do?"

"Crash dive, sir," was my reply.

"Exactly," says he. "That's just what happened. We are all down here together, U-boats and us. He can't depth charge us without making it damned uncomfortable for them."

So we crept away from the scene and remained down deep for the rest of the day. When darkness fell we went through the usual routine of surfacing, but, lo and behold, the skipper couldn't open the upper conning tower hatch, so he had to come down and go up the gun tower hatch. Then orders came down thick and fast. Second Coxswain and two ABs on the bridge, PO Telegraphist and a telegraphist on the bridge. Their task was to clear the debris as our bridge was a shambles. It was then that we realised we had got entangled with an explosive sweep. After some time spent hacking and sawing, they managed to free the upper conning tower hatch and tidy things up a bit. Then the working parties came back inside the boat.

After a short interval the captain's voice came down from the bridge: "Second Coxswain and two ABs to the bridge. Tell the First Lieutenant I've got a b . . . minesweeper in tow!"

Yes, we had torn another explosive sweep off a destroyer and had been towing it behind us ever since we had carried out our attack, but owing to the fact that we had stayed deep and took it down with us, we hadn't trailed it along on the surface flaunting it in Jerry's face. After a lot of hacking and sawing we managed to free that and cast it adrift. Being filled with explosive, we were mighty glad to be rid of it.

Everything passed off quietly for an hour or so and then we were summoned back to diving stations by the ringing of the night alarm. The lookouts had spotted a destroyer who passed us astern. There appeared to be a lot of activity from the enemy and the third officer informed us in the control room that the enemy was quite likely carrying out a box sweep and looking for us. The order was passed "Break the Charge. Half ahead together." This was no sooner accomplished than with a loud clatter one of the engines gave up the ghost. Throughout the remainder of the night we were on our toes, but we managed to remain undiscovered by the enemy, and with the coming dawn slid underneath the surface to continue our homeward

Flying her Jolly Roger, Tuna comes alongside the depot ship H.M.S. Forth.

passage and close our escort, who was still patiently waiting for us although we were many hours overdue at the rendezvous.

So terminated another patrol with our arrival back at base proudly showing our scars.

(Written by H. S. Roberts and originally published in SOCA (London Branch) Magazine for July, 1952. The U-boat sunk in this attack was the U644.

The Squeaker

The Squeaker was the code name given to a crystal receiver constructed by Petty Officer Telegraphist Charles Futer, of *Seal,* assisted by P.O. Tel. J. J. Nevitt of *Shark* while prisoners-of-war in Marlag Nord, a naval camp near Bremen. The fixed capacitor was made from pieces of tin and "borrowed" German film, the coil and aerial from the copper wire bindings of Canadian Red Cross parcels. The cat's whisker was a black market purchase and the 1000 ohm earpiece had at one time mysteriously vanished from a German telephone test set.

Tuning of the receiver was "by guess and by God." It was probably in the region of 49 metres and had meant many months of experimenting with coils of varying shapes and sizes. Tests took place perched up in an attic during severe winter weather. Success was finally achieved by the reception of a broadcast in German preceded by a "V" in morse code, which turned out to be the European broadcast news from England.

The Squeaker provided an adequate service for the twelve months leading up to D-Day. Shortly before June 6, 1944, a Dutch superhet valve receiver came into the possession of the news team. Long-wave coils were constructed for this new set in order to receive the Press News Service transmitted in morse by Rugby (GBR) on long wave. Full coverage of the news of the D-Day landings was given and a comprehensive service was maintained until the battle of the Falaise Gap.

Demand for news was so great that the team was operating for many hours daily. This led to laxity among the lookout teams and the two petty officer telegraphists were caught in the act and arrested by the Gestapo. It had become obvious to the Germans that there was a radio in the camp. During one of their searches they had entered a room to be confronted by a large map on the wall, with an inscription underneath saying "As per B.B.C., not German bulls..."

Under interrogation the team claimed to have been given this Dutch wireless set by Able Seaman Joe Coleman (he had lost an arm in *Shark's* action against the Luftwaffe in July, 1940). The interrogator sneeringly remarked: "So when you are in trouble you would rat on your comrade to save your own skin." This officer then dashed back to the camp to arrest A. B. Coleman, quite forgetting that Joe had already been exchanged for a similarly disabled U-boat seaman some months previously. A returning guard whispered, once the penny had dropped: "The Herr Leutnant is not pleased with you." However, the two petty officers stuck doggedly to their original story in spite of rigorous interrogation lasting many weeks.

The Germans were intrigued by the long-wave coils, maintaining that these converted the receiver into a transmitter. When Charlie Futer said he had no idea what the coils could be used for, he was told: told: "We know that the British Admiralty only employ bloody fools as funkmeisters (P.O. Tels)." During one interrogation "Drip" Nevitt was bothered by the sight of a pair of boots peeping from an alcove. His anxious glances in that direction were invariably frustrated by a corrective thump on his right ear from the Feldwebel standing behind him. The prisoner was being questioned as to how they managed to key the set for transmitting purposes. His answers being unsatisfactory, he was dragged over to the set and his face was pushed into it, but not before he had a quick glance at the owner of the boots. It was not a feared "trigger man", only the figure of an old friend, "Albert R.N.," the famous dummy used in naval officer escapes.

Unbeknown to the two P.O. Tels the camp commandant, Kapitan zur See Schmidt, had immediately contacted the German Admiralty on hearing of their arrest. He claimed it was a matter for them to deal with and not the Gestapo. The two prisoners were eventually charged with having committed a severe breach of German Naval Discipline, namely, they had been in improper possession of a Dutch wireless set and had used it for listening to "enemy propaganda." The actual supplier of the set, a German civilian black marketeer, was executed later in 1944 for his activities but the Gestapo apparently never discovered his connection in the matter.

Having served their sentences in solitary confinement, the news team brought the Squeaker back into service, but kept it strictly for the nightly reception of the broadcast in German from England. When the camp was evacuated in the face of the advancing British Army in the spring of 1945, the naval prisoners-of-war were forced on the road and marched east. The Gestapo were not very impressed with the Navy's efforts at route marching (only four miles were covered on the first day), so on passing through Zeven, they enlisted the help of 150 S.S. police. In spite of the column being attacked by Spitfires (clearing the road for British armoured units), the team managed to provide an adequate service with the Squeaker. One of these Spitfire attacks, at Seedorf, resulted in the death of that very gallant naval officer, Commander B. G. Scurfield, O.B.E., D.S.O., A.M., of *H.M.S. Bedouin,* besides other casualties.

The naval column was usually put into a field for the night which would just happen to be adjacent to some strategic crossroads or railway junction. These were inviting targets for the R.A.F. Mosquito bombers, even though the Germans would personally lay out the sign "R.A.F. P.o.Ws" in a prominent position. That never worked either. A handy tree could usually be found for the aerial and the faithful Squeaker was in operation every night. One particular night's billet posed problems – it was a stone quarry. Two short sticks were found, the aerial wire strung between them and a tatty old blanket hung up to dry. One of the guards congratulated the team on their efforts to dry the blanket.

The most comfortable billet, one rainy night, was a cold frame in a back garden. With a lovely warm layer of old horse manure and a glass roof and the aerial hitched to the garden fence, it was business as usual. An officer who was part of the R.A.F. column nightly broke away from his own party in order to get the gen provided by the crystal set. The first time he contacted the team, the set was being operated in the bottom of a turnip trench, with his own Mosquito bombers overhead. Apart from expressing amazement that the crystal set actually worked, he also had to admit rather ruefully that in spite of his having the latest thing in radio reception – "acorn valves" – his set was useless without power. One item of news during this period was the discovery by British troops of the extermination camp at Belsen. Oddly enough, it was only a few miles to the west of the naval camp, but none of the prisoners-of-war knew of its existence.

The final news bulletin received by the Squeaker was on arrival of the column at the S.S. police barracks at Bad Soltau. Radio reception was poor in the quarters assigned to the P.o.W.s so the team was obliged to operate in the attic of the tallest building available. Underneath were billeted the S.S. units who had been guarding the prisoners during their march. By this time their beloved Fuehrer had committed suicide and by the "zombie" look on their faces, they were probably past caring. The naval column were released by the 11th Armoured Division on May 2, 1945. P.O. Futer brought his baby home.

Mad Dogs and Englishmen

or Are Submariners Nutty?

Place: Ployarnoe Submarine Base, North Russia.

Time: Mid-winter, 1941-42.

Participants: Duty Watch Fore-endsmen.

We decided it was about time we showed the Russian sentries, in their very thick clothing and comfortable tents at the end of the jetty, just how tough British submariners really were so we decided to show them by ditching the gash.

There were four of us and we stripped to our chain breakers, casually sauntering up the gangplank on to the jetty. We remained there for about half a minute, talking, smiling and laughing, then very slowly walked below to the astonishment of the onlookers. However, they should have seen the scene below as we pushed and shoved, our teeth chattering, to get nearer the electric fire. No sign of cameraderie there, of course, we were bonkers – had to be in wartime.

Summer Wars

Lurking down at thirty feet
With some on watch and some asleep
This way, that way, back and forth
Sometimes South'rd, sometimes North.

"Permission to shake the next watch on?"
"Yes please messenger, carry on."
For'd then to shake the crew
And then return to make a brew.

First shake "Guns", and then shake "Ping"
A grunt from one and then they sing.
"Jesus Christ! This makes yer weep,
We've only just managed to fall asleep."

A quarter past, still no relief,
Back I steal like a sneaking thief,
There to find when I get back
They've turned around on the other tack!

Shaken again they wake with starts.
"Come on Red Watch have a heart."
One tumbles out, then two, then three,
And hopefully, inquire for tea.

The radar voices on the line
Pinpoint an echo at Red Two Nine.
Ping's dripping voice still moaning low
Settles for "HE, red three O."

The skipper puts on a little spurt,
Jimmy looks a trifle hurt
And pointedly inquires from aft
The amount of juice left in the craft.

"Vessel in contact," comes from Ping
"Damn and blast the bloody thing.
"One hundred feet!" the skipper swears.
The boat descends the liquid stairs.

Silence now all quiet within,
A hacking cough's a deadly sin.
From up above the search goes on,
All our chance of sleep seems gone.

When suddenly the silence ceased,
Charges shattered the ocean's peace.
The only frown in the CR space
Was written on the skipper's face.

Once more "up top" for a laugh and joke,
The first fag won't be much to smoke,
But we've four more hours in which to snore
Till starting again this bloodless war.

So to this ode I'll add no more,
Maybe we'll settle that little score.
We're praying like hell for that run ashore,
But until then "Press on."

Then one by one, they trundle aft,
Some look blank, the others daft.
Jimmy looks on with mild concern,
Too many hands are passing astern.

The L.T.O.s are passing now.
Demented, Jimmy no more can row.
His eyes burn fire, his lips draw thin.
"Bang goes my latest bloody trim."

The boat begins to rock about,
Jimmy the One begins to shout
And works into a seething sweat,
The gunlayer chuckles in his "set."

A vessel sighted off the bow
Creates a bigger "Bull and Cow."
The klaxon gives two warning screams
Frightened, hands awake from dreams.

The skipper by now has joined the fray
Trying to sight them through the spray,
And looking swiftly at depth and trim
Wishes to Christ he was still "turned in."

The bubble wanders fore and aft
Displaying our cigar-shaped craft.
In frantic movements passing fore
A lift in some department store

The captain orders "Forty feet,"
Jimmy attempts this hazardous feat,
And bless his heart he's done it too
The skipper sighs "Oh, well done blue."

Jimmy by now has gained his trim,
The skipper with glee is filled to the brim,
While "Navvie" expectantly is seen
Edging towards the fruit machine.

ABOVE: Lieut-Commander G.C. Phillips, of H.M.S. Ursula, returns to Blyth after his attack on the German cruiser Leipzig in December, 1939. He was awarded the D.S.O. and promoted shortly afterwards. He earned the gratitude of thousands of submariners for his invention of the so-called Ursula suit, a waterproof affair which replaced the traditional heavy oilskins and sou'wester. BELOW: Wren Marjorie Harris at work on Ursula at H.M.S. Dolphin, Gosport, after the boat's return from the Mediterranean.

Unswerving

From the diary of E.R.A. Peter Forbes, temporarily drafted to *Unswerving* in 1944.

July 31, 1944. Left Malta for patrol – where we don't know yet. My first patrol on a "U" class boat. Very easy engine room watch.

August 1. Still on the surface. The food here is far superior to what we get at base. Had two fresh eggs already; two more than we've had ashore in three months.

August 2. Dived all day, then surfaced at 2100. We had just got up when the klaxon went. Dive again, then the order to shut off for depth charging. The captain had just opened the top lid and looked around and had seen a kayak and two escorts. They were very near and had seen us. The asdic is no good, absolutely dead, so our ears are cut off when we are dived and we must trust to luck. Well, 16 charges dropped and I was a bit shaky waiting on the first one, being away from the sea for so long but I was all right then. Surfaced an hour later and they were 7,000 yards away. They didn't see us so we charged our batteries, which were low.

August 3. Nothing happened all day. Surfaced at night at the same time but had to dive three times between 2300 and 2400 becaue of aircraft: maybe out looking for us. Then had to dive again at 0300. Tried to work on the asdic to repair it but it's no good at all. That means we are at a great disadvantage for the rest of the patrol.

August 5. Surfaced at 1400, the middle of the afternoon, cruising around the islands just out of sight of land. We expected to be forced down again but nothing saw us. We are making our way around the islands of Greece.

August 6. Nearly in the Gulf of Athens. Haven't seen a thing so far but I don't mind at all. It ain't no picnic to get a pattern of depth charges on you.

August 7. Still a quiet patrol, taking photographs of a radar station ashore through the periscope.

August 9. About 0230 this morning, night alarm went and we had to stand by to dive as an enemy plane was flying about too near to be comfortable. Then our RDF picked up a ship's engines a good few miles away so we put on full speed to catch this ship, and it turns out to be only 500 tons so we go to gun action stations. She hadn't seen us and we were at extreme range with our three-inch. We had only fired six rounds when she opened up on us with four 3.7in. guns. What a shock to us, a submarine-detecting boat. We had no more chance keeping on the surface so we turned right round and put our tail between our legs and beat it as fast as our motors could take us with shells flying all around us. But we got out of her range and nothing eventful happened the remaining hours of the night or during the day.

August 10. Yesterday afternoon we received a message telling us about a convoy that passed through another of our submarine billets. A m/v of 780 and an escort of one destroyer and an "R" boat (an enlargement of our MLs). The other submarine has sunk the destroyer. We made for a position that the remaining members of the convoy would be in at dawn, but we picked them up on the RDF during the night and followed them, plotting their course, trying to get details of their zigzag.

We dived at dawn and the enemy were just on the horizon. We kept at action stations and went to full ahead on the motors. When we were in a position of about 800 yards, the captain got ready for his attack when suddenly the R boat came racing towards us and forced us down to 60 feet. We thought it had discovered us, but no. We went full ahead again to get in another attacking position. Eventually we had the target right and the torpedoes at the ready. Then about a minute and a half later, about 1,200 yards away, there were two dull thuds followed by successive explosions. We had got two hits, so we shut off for depth charging. You imagine the people on the ship doing their jobs with no idea of the cylinders of death coming towards them – they had loved ones, too. Then the waiting for the charges is trying on the nerves. Eventually one dropped, not near at all. They dropped five in all and only the last two were fairly near. No more dropped so we went to breakfast. We had earned it I think even though it was only a small ship. "Exit Toni."

August 12. Nothing has happened since we started on the road back at noon today. At 2000 tonight we started to dive under a minefield at 200 feet, surfaced again at 2200. Hope we keep on the surface all the way.

August 15. Returned to Malta after a very quiet patrol, quite a contrast from when I was on *Trooper,* when patrols were longer, food scarce and convoys with plenty of escorts. It was a rest cure for me after the hard work in the Spare Crew.

Timoshenko

by Joe Lewis

Unruffled was on her way to join the 10th Flotilla in Malta. The date was July, 1942, when she passed Gibraltar during her working-up trials. The P.O. Tel. was walking through the dockyard when he was approached by a Wren (not the feathered type, I hasten to add, but a real-live pretty girl). Thinking his luck had changed at last, he paused but had his hopes dashed when she produced this tiny bundle of fur and requested a home for it. That was how the cat joined the Royal Navy in general and *Unruffled* in particular. He was welcomed aboard by all hands, made an absolute idiot of, and named after the gallant Russian Marshal Timoshenko.

If there is anything in the belief of transmigration, then Timoshenko had been a submariner before, and an outside wrecker to boot, for he made his dining station under the control panel, where he would yawn and mew when a fish left the tube. He was quickly "house" trained and used to do his "georges," as the Captain (Lieut. J. Stevens) quaintly called them, in a box in the P.O.s' mess. Should he forget himself at any time, there was always a willing hand to use the heads and blow the indiscretion over the side.

Timmo, as he quickly became known, accompanied *Unruffled* on every one of her patrols and was awarded a collar with a silver plate bearing his name. It was widely recognised that most of the cat world along Gzira front owed their existence to Timmo's eye for a pretty cat. One sure thing was that on arriving in from patrol, Timmo would disappear for two or three days, returning with what one can only described as a satisfied smirk on his face.

Timmo gave us a scare when he fell ill and we discovered it was cat flu and prepared for the worst. A vet looked him over, however, diagnosed a chill and gave me Friars Balsam and the method of treatment. This gentleman, whose name we didn't know, refused to accept a fee, but he earned forever the gratitude of *Unruffled.* Timoshenko was soon his old self again. Will anybody who saw the fight ever forget the routing of the Alsatian dog in the Lazaretto? I certainly won't. I thought our brave lad was a goner until, yelping with pain, the dog bolted, leaving the field to Timmo.

Came the day when we were due to leave for patrol. No cat – panic stations. Searches revealed nothing! Captain (S) ordered that *Unruffled* was not to sail without her cat and a search of all boats was instituted. He was found in the P.O.s' mess of a boat that shall be nameless. Suffice it to say they were just passing through and not of the 10th Flotilla.

Our spell of duty over, we headed west and Timmo found himself back in the land of his birth. He developed a daily routine during our stay in Gibraltar. After breakfast he would go ashore and not be seen again until about 1700, when he would settle down for the night. Our final departure from Gib was timed for 1300 so it was plain that if we couldn't keep him on the boat we would lose him. The First Lieutenant (Lieut. O. Lascelles) suggested that we secure him to the gun and this was done. A miserable creature of a killick L.T.O. said that was no way to treat a cat and set him loose. Goodbye, Timoshenko. I think I can paraphrase the poet and say:

Hail to thee, Blithe Spirit,
Cat thou never were!

He was succeeded by Timoshenko II and III but neither of these appraoched the Master and I'm sure all old Unruffleds will agree with me when I say: "No cat ever will."

Ultimatum's crew relax with their Jolly Roger. This boat survived the war after claiming a German U-boat and an Italian submarine.

The Manx Camel

by Tomsig

Throughout naval history, many ships' captains have been presented with gifts by local dignitaries in many parts of the world, as a diplomatic courtesy or more often for services rendered in troubled times. The gifts when proferred may not be refused, no matter what the shape or size.

Witness the case of *Trident* and *Tigris,* operating with the Russians, who presented the boats with baby reindeer. By the time they returned to Holy Loch, their antlers had grown to such an extent that the "babies" could not be hauled up through the fore hatch. The problem was solved with simple ingenuity by the Outside Wrecker, who hacksawed the antlers down to size.

Other navies had similar problems. When the German U339 and U274 operated along the North African coast in 1942-43, a local Arab sheik presented the senior officer, Kapitan Willi Fischer, with a fine baby racing camel. Due to the baby's hump, there was no question of loading it down the fore hatch, and the boat could not very well dive with the animal on the casing without offending the sheik's highly developed sense of protocol. As the boats were on a secret gun-running job under the noses of the Allies, surface running would be sure to attract unwelcome attention.

In the true fashion of chain of command, "See to it, Number One" was translated into "I think it's an engineering job," and as the job was upper deck, it was quickly placed in the capable hands of the German equivalent of the Outside Wrecker and Second Scratch. In real Heath Robinson style, comprising lumps of ginger string, strops and shackles, the camel's nose was shackled to the for'ard jumping wire, its tail to the muzzle of the four-inch gun, while its legs were strapped down to the upper deck grilles. This kept the camel neatly in line fore and aft so that at a suitable place further down the coast and out of sight of the Arabs, the boat could edge inshore, release the strops and toggles, and the baby would presumably swim off towards the Sahara.

U339, being the junior boat, said "Auf Wiedersehen" and slid away westwards into the gathering dusk to resume her patrol, leaving U274 to proceed in an opposite direction along the coast. As she could not dive, nor go to full buoyancy, the boat steamed along at what became known as "Camel depth."

"Surely the British will see us?"

"I don't think so," replied the Kapitan. No self-respecting officer of the watch on the bridge of a destroyer is going to risk court martial by reporting to his C.O: "Sir, there's a camel trimmed down on the starboard bow."

Then disaster struck as U274 rounded the headland. Out of the gloom at a fierce rate of knots appeared an Allied fast patrol craft. Willi Fischer quickly realised that torpedo action was out of the question and promptly ordered: "Night alarm, gun action." Within seconds, the gun's crew had loaded, trained, laid and got one away, scoring a direct hit on the after part of the patrol craft, which turned away belching smoke and flames, no doubt both shocked and surprised by the apparition of a trimmed down camel.

Gun layers in the German submarine service, it would appear, are no less characters than their British equivalent, and in this action paid scant attention to the feelings of the camel. In training the gun, he wrenched away the posterial fitments, probably inflicting painful damage on the associated external orifice into the bargain. Such was the force upon the camel that the quick release strops and toggles and the ginger string pulled away, and the baby plunged over the side to disappear landward into the dark Mediterranean night. To this day, the legend persists among certain Arab tribes of the herd of Manx camels.

Spirit

There are no battlefields to remind you,
No torn landscape, wreckage or mass graves.
Our battlefield was 'neath the oceans
Where we fought for freedom's ways.

There are no pilgrimages, wreaths or anniversaries,
Few survivors have our tale to tell.
We couldn't hide or run away
But we went and fought, and died as well.

To all that follow in our wake
Let our spirit your guiding light be.
If you dive in anger, remember, we are with you
And this is your might, you'll see.

As it was with us, Drake and Nelson
And you with us all three.
No-one can defeat you
In the silent battle 'neath the sea.

ABOVE: Flying her Jolly Roger with the White Ensign beneath it, Saracen cuts a fine dash en route to Algiers in 1943, with Lieut. M.G.R. Lumby in command. She was lost off Corsica a few months later, with a U-boat and an Italian submarine to her credit. BELOW: Talisman on stand-easy at Halifax, Nova Scotia.

The End of H.M. Submarine Shark

The following is a statement made by the Commanding Officer of *Shark,* Lieut.-Commander P. N. Buckley, R.N., after his release from prisoner-of-war camp in 1945, concerning the loss of his submarine.

Friday, July 5, 1940.

A very rough day, blowing hard from the westward with a heavy westerly swell. Nothing was seen or heard during the day. I decided to surface at 2200 for the following reasons:

(a) We were in a comparatively safe position (so I thought) about 30 miles from Skudesnes bearing 230.

(b) The battery was low having done a long day's diving in a rough sea.

(c) We had been ordered to patrol off the entrance to the fiord on July 6 and 7 and it would therefore be impossible to charge for any length of time on the following night.

(d) As there was never any darkness at this time of year in these latitudes, it would be at its darkest about 2230.

(e) Nothing had been seen or heard during the day.

On surfacing, the starboard engine was got under way and I ordered 60-degree zigs every five minutes and a 180-degree turn after ten minutes at a speed of eight knots on the starboard engine, with a standing charge on the port side. A delay occurred with the port engine due to a leaky blast air connection to No. 6 P and in fact the charge was never started.

At 2215, when on a course of about 230, the lookout reported a seaplane right astern. The bridge was cleared and the submarine dived immediately. There was a delay on the starboard side, unaccounted for, and the boat was slow in diving due, I presumed at the time, to being head-on to the heavy swell. The control room depth gauge was reading something between 15 and 20 feet when two or three bombs fell very close to the stern, followed immediately by two or three more which shook the boat violently. Considerable damage was done by these explosions – lights were put out, Sperry went off the board and both hydroplanes and steering failed. The starboard main motor was also out of action and an electric fire started behind it. The HP air line aft of the ER bulkhead "started" so the line was isolated at the bulkhead. There was a leak behind the port main motor switchboard and water was coming in at this place. The after planes were jammed "hard a rise" and could not be moved in either power or hand.

The boat now took up an angle of about 35 degrees "bow up" and the bow broke surface, in spite of having filled all possible tanks and attempting to lighten the boat aft. The port main motor was worked at full speed. As soon as the bow broke surface a hail of machine gun bullets was heard on the hull and bombs were dropped around us.

After what seemed an incredibly long period (it was probably not more than a minute or two) the boat at last began to gain depth, although at the same angle by the stern. As soon as we were reasonably deep I commenced to trim on main ballast, but with no result. Whenever the speed of the port main motor was altered the boat took up a greater angle and it was impossible to run at a slower speed than full ahead, group up. The after main ballast tanks were completely emptied with no apparent effect on the angle. The boat continued to gain depth rapidly in spite of all efforts to frustrate it. It was now reported that the HP air was very low and that water was coming in aft (the battery I knew to be very low) so that when the control room gauge showed 210 feet, I decided to use all remaining air in an attempt to bring the boat to the surface and try to get away under what cover of night there might be. By blowing all main tanks she started to rise at 256 feet by the control room gauge and 320 aft. The boat surfaced at an incredible angle and most of the gear that had not already done so during the initial dive took charge. I felt almost certain that due to cracked containers a great deal of acid from the batteries had been spilled and this afterwards proved to be true. On reaching the surface there was only 750lb. per square inch of HP air remaining.

We got under way on the starboard engine immediately, the time now being about 2245, and using the port main motor half ahead group up until the port engine could be made ready, I attempted to set a westerly course in order to take us clear from the land. My object was to carry out a detailed inspection of the damage, although I was satisfied that a further dive was impossible.

The main aerial abaft the bridge had been carried away, but the P.O. Tel eventually rigged a jury aerial and a signal T.O.O. 22.50 was sent asking for assistance. The port engine was very stiff to blow over and it appeared as though the bearings aft of the engine room were considerably out of line. Eventually she started but it was found impossible to obtain more than 260 revs.

It was now that we discovered for certain real damage which finally sealed our fate. The rudder was jammed "hard a port". Attempts were made to steer by main engines but unfortunately all efforts failed as the port engine would not go fast enough to counteract the effect of the rudder in spite of slowing down, and on one occasion of stopping, the starboard engine.

The situation at approximately 2315 was therefore as follows:

1. We were on the surface and unable to dive.
2. With the steering gear out of action we had no alternative but to proceed in circles to port of varying diameter. This was made possible by altering the revs of the starboard engine as much as possible, although it was deemed inadvisable to stop the engine for more than was absolutely necessary on account of the shortage of air.
3. A signal had been sent asking for assistance.

4. It was to all intents and purposes broad daylight with no chance of visibility decreasing.

5. The after ends were flooded to a level over the shafts.

6. All lubricating had been washed from the Plummer and Thrust bearings.

7. The ballast pump was running at full and not keeping the leak in hand.

8. The stern was twisted to starboard for about 20 feet aft and opened back from the after escape chamber.

9. Both propeller guards were shattered.

10. A very large dent in pressure hull over after ends.

11. There was a leak behind the port main motor panel.

12. A split jacket on the starboard group exhaust valve wedging was employed and the flow of water circulating into engine room was thus restricted.

13. No. 1 battery was showing signs of overheating and giving off dense fumes and smoke. No. 1 battery fuses were therefore dropped but had little effect in reducing the smoke.

14. Most electrical circuits, including Sperry, were out of action. The circulating pump starters failed from time to time and were eventually held on by the judicious use of string.

15. The port shaft was apparently out of line.

The gun was manned and all HA ammunition was brought on deck. Lewis gun and all rifles were manned on the bridge as we were determined to use all available means of having a crack at the enemy, and, if possible, to hold them off until help arrived. Below demolition charges were rigged in the torpedo compartment and the A/S office and all CBs and secret charts were prepared for destruction. Weighted books were thrown over the side (the depth of the water being in the vicinity of 130 fathoms), whilst other books and charts were torn into minute fragments and burnt in the conning tower. I am confident that none of these could possibly have been compromised.

About midnight we were spotted and we were subjected to continuous bombing attacks. The first attack was very close and one bomb which exploded on the starboard side holed four main ballast as well as washing two men over the side. The boat now listed heavily to starboard. We kept fairly upright by running the blower and admitting water to the port tanks, but I was reluctant to do this as we were losing buoyancy the whole time due to the leaks aft and in the engine room.

During the action a Heinkel seaplane was used as a marker. She flew round us the whole time keeping up a steady fire with her cannon, but this appeared to be ineffective although many rounds hit the pressure hull. We set the HA ammunition at the lowest fuse setting and concentrated on keeping the Heinkel at a reasonable range with the gun, whilst the Lewis gun and rifles were used against the planes when making bombing attacks.

At some time or other – I am afraid "times" throughout are only very approximate – shouts were heard coming from the water close to us and we soon recognised Eaton and Pain, i.e. the two who had fallen overboard during the first attack. Although I was doubtful as to whether we could start the engines again I decided to stop and pick

Shark's crew prepare to leave their stricken submarine.

them up as there appeared to be a slight lull in the bombing attacks. This evolution was completed without incident and Eaton and Pain were rescued. They were still in wonderful spirits although obviously tired. Later on they helped in the excellent work that was done by the crew.

About 0130 I realised that I had made a mistake in giving a course and speed in my signals as it would mislead the authorities into thinking that we had made good our escape. As the attacks were now getting more frequent and the seaplane was not going to allow us to get out of sight, I ordered an amplifying signal in plain language to be sent. All the efforts of the P.O. Tel were in vain, however, as the W/T office breakers would not "hold on". The fuses to No. 1 battery had been dropped owing to fire having started in the tank some time previously and No. 2 battery was producing 350 volts. This remarkable voltage was eventually reduced to 286 volts by dropping the fuses of every circuit not absolutely essential, but still the breakers would not hold on. The load could not be read as all the ammeters were out of action.

The wardroom and engine room were by now full of smoke and fumes from the battery (the torpedo room and after ends had been isolated by the bulkhead doors) and the water level in the engine room was rising, so that from now on it was necessary to change over the pump suction from the after ends to the engine room and vice versa in order to get the best results.

It was now necessary to clear the magazine of all ammunition as the wardroom was becoming rapidly untenable. This was done personally by the First Lieutenant, using a DSEA set as a gas mask. Working in the magazine under these conditions was extremely unpleasant but was completely successfully, although all workers had to take several breathers under the conning tower hatch before they could continue.

Great work was also being done by the engine room staff in keeping the engines running and altering the revs on the starboard engine. It was deemed inadvisable to touch the port engine at all after she had been started. The engine room was choking with fumes and conditions were very bad, but the engineer officer and two of his E.R.A.s managed successfully to deal with the situations as they arose, spending any spare time under the conning tower hatch getting breaths of fresh air until either an engine movement was necessary or some fresh contingency had to be met and overcome.

On deck the gun, Lewis gun and rifles were manned and the remainder of the crew were employed as supply parties and, most essential, in filling the Lewis gun pans as they became empty. This latter was a whole-time job as, on practically every occasion of a bombing attack being carried out, the contents of a small pan would be exhausted.

During an attack, one HA shell exploded close under the stern of a Dornier which made off towards Stavanger with sparks coming from it, amid loud cheers from *Shark's* crew, who naturally assumed that it had been hit. It is quite possible that this might have been the case.

About 0245 Petty Officer J. S. Gibson fell over the side and was never seen again. This was a sad blow to everyone, as he was a very competent P.O. who had shown his real merits under active service conditions. I cannot say what caused him to fall overboard, but it is probable that he was killed outright by one of the bullets that were flying around at this time.

Some time about 0300, four Messerschmitt 109's appeared from the direction of Stavanger and from now on continued to rake the bridge and guns' crews with machine gun and cannon fire. Their fire was devastating and it was obvious to me that the end was now in sight although everyone stuck to their posts in a magnificent manner until wounded or, in one case, killed outright.

One of the seaplanes now signalled us by light to "Stop or steer towards Stavanger". No notice was taken of this signal but about a quarter of an hour later, after continuous attacks from the 109's, our ammunition being expended and having many wounded or dead (I could not tell which), I reluctantly decided to capitulate.

Some time after the "fighter" attacks had commenced I called the First Lieutenant on to the bridge as I was feeling particularly shaky, and, from this time on, I have only a vague recollection as to what actually happened, so that the remainder of the narrative is supplied by the First Lieutenant and other officers.

Nearly all our casualties were sustained during the attacks of the ME's and at the finish the bridge was a shambles of wounded men, blood and empty cartridge cases. Stoker Walsh had been killed outright. After we had been lying stopped for about half an hour, one of the small seaplanes landed close astern of us and the two airmen eventually came aboard. Shortly after this their plane broke adrift, heeled over and sank. They explained that they had been hit in one of the floats during the action but I think it is more probable that they damaged one of their floats when landing and did not like to admit it. The pilot and observer appeared very nervous and the former was particularly loth to remove his finger from the trigger of his Luger pistol. These two were quite content to remain on the bridge, so there was ample opportunity for the First Lieutenant and officers to go below for the purpose of destroying everything which might have been of interest to the Germans. Wounded men were laid out on the gun platform as the atmosphere inside the boat had now become almost impossible.

Everything was now ready for blowing up and sinking the boat and the exact moment at which to take this step was the question which exercised my mind in view of the large number of wounded on board. To my mind there was no point in doing it until there was any likelihood of the boat being taken "in toto", and this would not be possible until some form of surface craft had arrived fairly close to the boat, when there would be a reasonable chance of the wounded being picked up. As events turned out, the First Lieutenant, in my absence, was able to get all the crew to safety and sink the boat in very deep water, a very praiseworthy effort.

About 0500 one of the large seaplanes landed and two officers came aboard in a rubber boat. After a great deal of manoeuvering I was eventually got on board the seaplane, where my leg and head were made as comfortable as possible. I was joined about half an hour later by Sub-Lieut. Barnes, R.N.R., and we took off for Stavanger about 0615. When we left, *Shark* was lying very low in the water, stern down and I was certain that she would sink shortly. Seaplanes, bombers and fighters were flying around and, when we left, the gallant *Shark* was at the mercy of at least ten hostile aircraft.

On board all settled down to wait. The wounded, who were fit to move, were on the gun tower, with their dressings renewed as long as supplies lasted. Rum and cigarettes were issued to those without head wounds. DSEA sets were fitted on the helpless.

Throughout the action all officers and men had displayed great courage and the spirit of the crew remained excellent to the end. The way in which the Lewis gun and rifles were manned on the bridge was an example to all. The gun's crew, supplemented by the supply parties, stood up to all the attacks without flinching. Although various members have been singled out for praise, all behaved in a most admirable manner.

During the wait, all loose gear such as grenades, small arms and three-inch ammunition was ditched and the control room, W/T and A/S cabinets were broken up. The engine room was by now flooding and the boat was appreciably lower in the water and rolling very sluggishly in the westerly swell. Eventually, about 0730, smoke was sighted in the direction of Stavanger which was soon apparent to be that of four trawlers. These arrived about 0830. One trawler secured alongside the starboard side and two the port side. The wounded were all transferred to the trawlers and were attended by a Surgeon Lieutenant, who had been sent out specially.

At 0930 the trawlers set off and two of them attempted to tow *Shark*. Practically immediately afterwards, the tow was cut as *Shark* was sinking. She went down vertically, stern first, and her last action was to damage the propeller of one of the trawlers, so that in the end, it was one of our enemy trawlers and not *Shark* which was towed back to Stavanger. She sank some 30 miles south-west of Stavanger in about 700 feet of water.

Besides activities carried out on board, the following steps were taken to ensure that she did not fall into enemy hands:

1. The main battery outboard and inboard ventilation systems were opened up throughout the boat.

2. "A" inboard vent was left open, with the object of slowly flooding forward. Water was coming in forward and some unknown degree of damage had been sustained, presumably by bombs.

3. Before the engine room was evacuated, the strongback of the engine room hatch was removed, hatch opened and dropped back with dogs to shut. When the trawlers were sighted, the level of water was above the door sill and the ballast pump was stopped.

4. When the last of the wounded was taken from the bridge the telemotor by-pass was opened. Pressure on the panel was lost in a minute or so and the vents were only kept shut by the air pressure in the tanks. This was observed to be leaking satisfactorily as the Engineer Officer left the bridge.

5. Main and auxiliary panels were opened up with levers to "shut".

Round Trip

When the second stick of depth charges exploded around H.M. Submarine *Shark* off Skudesnes Fiord, south-west of Norway, on the evening of July 6, 1940, she floundered to the surface at an incredible angle. The lights were out, the starboard main motor was stopped, a fire was blazing behind it and water was pouring in through a leak. As the rudder was jammed hard a-port, *Shark* could only go round in circles. A jury aerial was rigged and Lieut.-Commander P.N. Buckley, R.N., sent off the message "Unable to dive; 58-51 N 04-50 E; need assistance," but he knew there was little hope of it reaching them in time.

After running submerged all day ready to surface and flash instant warning if a German invasion fleet sailed from Stavanger, *Shark* had been spotted by a German plane when she surfaced at 2230 to try to charge batteries. She had been seen all too clearly in the half light which persists during the summer months off Norway. For more than three hours the submariners fought back gallantly and even raised a cheer when one of their three-inch shells sent a Heinkel seaplane limping away with sparks shooting out of its tail, but then four ME109 fighters poured a hail of fire into the decks and conning tower. Two of the crew were killed and 19 others, including the captain, were wounded.

Fifteen minutes later the submarine ran out of ammunition and the captain, himself wounded in the head and leg, reluctantly decided to break off the action. The crew of the first seaplane to board the *Shark* were left stranded when their plane sank through a riddled float. While a second seaplane alighted and took off the captain, the First Lieutenant, Lieut. D. H. B. Barratt, R.N., completed scuttling preparations. When three armed trawlers arrived, took off the crew and the airmen, and tried to tow *Shark* away, she sank suddenly. Her bow hit the propeller of one of the trawlers and the vessel had to be towed back to base.

So Lieut.-Commander Buckley, his officers and the crew of the *Shark* passed into German captivity. The submariners were at various camps. One was E.R.A. Frederick William Edmond Hammond, R.N., who was determined to escape. In the spring of 1942 he was at Marlag Nord, Sandbostel, near Hamburg. Here he became friends with Donald Lister, a fellow E.R.A. from submarines and a kindred spirit. Hammond, short, thickset, neat and sharp-eyed, was known to everyone as Wally. Lister, taller, stouter, easy going and with a lively sense of humour, was universally known as Tubby. He had been a prisoner since May, 1940, from the submarine *Seal* which had hit a mine in the Kattegat after laying mines of her own and had lain on the seabed for many hours. She had struggled to the surface with a sick and exhausted crew and was further damaged by German planes while Lieut-Commander R. P. Lonsdale was trying to reach Sweden. With all her secret papers and gear destroyed, the partly-flooded *Seal* had been boarded by the Germans but British and Germans soon abandoned the boat and left her to sink. Though heeled over far to port and heavily down by the stern, *Seal* stayed afloat and so just reached Denmark on the end of a German towline. The Germans repaired the boat but learned little from her and were never able to make much use of her.

In April, 1942, the two E.R.A. s tunnelled out of Sandbostel, but were caught at Hamburg. Sent to the fortress prison of Colditz Castle, south of Leipzig in Saxony (now in East Germany), they got out of Oflag IVc by "complaining" of being put in an officers' camp, and by getting the officers to complain of other ranks being put in with them. As other ranks the E.R.A.s agreed vaguely to "work for Germany" and the gates of Colditz eventually opened. Meanwhile the very officers who had "complained" forged identity papers, provided money and briefed the E.R.A.s with all available information. The escapers were to be Flemish diesel engineers working as collaborators in Germany. They were to acquire their escape gear as the opportunity offered and were eventually to head for the Swiss border by a route followed by other Colditz escapers.

Transferred to Stalag VIIIb at Lamsdorf, near Breslau Gas Works, in Silesia, the escapers got an R.S.M. Sheriff to draft them to work in the gas works sidings. While a Sergeant Brown obtained clothes, Hammond and Lister shfited one small heap of coal about the yard and saw that shunting engines ran over the electric cables of a crane grab. Sergeant Brown obtained the clothes and enough food was found for the escapers to take with them. Leaving a dummy grave of coal slack in the yard, surmounted by a wooden cross marked "Adolph R.I.P.," the escapers prepared to vanish into the night of December 12, 1942.

When a sentry appeared at the escape position, Hammond and Lister gave out that the escape was off, then volunteered to wash up the Sunday soup cauldrons in the wash house. Hiding their civilian clothes in the cauldrons they changed in the wash house and slipped out through the gas works manager's garden. In a suitcase and a briefcase they carried food, shaving gear, mending things and bottle of mixture for Hammond's smoker's cough.

They travelled by tram to Breslau station, then by train to join the Colditz escape route at Dresden, smoking meerschaum pipes and showing German cigarettes. They passed through all police checks quickly, except when one officer lingered over checking their papers "because two prisoners had escaped." Going via Nuremburg they continued to Ulm, accepting a drink from a German soldier along the way. They were diesel engineers called to Rottweil to repair an engine while they were returning to Belgium for Christmas. All travellers to Rottweil had to change trains at Tuttlingen, which was only 15 miles from the Swiss border.

Getting to Ulm on Tuesday night, they found there was no train until morning. There was sleet and rain, but the escapers could not stay in the railway station. After trying to walk about the countryside they got a room at a cheap hotel in Ulm. The only other language which the manager spoke was English so they "understood a little bit of this," and checked that the Rottweil train left at 10 a.m. After breakfasting on their own bread, margarine and sugar they could not

E.R.A.s Hammond (left) and Lister in Switzerland after talking their way out of Colditz. They were the only British submariners to escape from Germany and make their way back to Britain during the war.

resist pouring water into a German officer's jackboots standing outside another room. On the train to Tuttlingen they returned the stares of an inquisitive German woman until she got off the train in embarrassment.

Walking half a mile from Tuttlingen station at 4 p.m., they were stopped by a police patrol. The officer was not entirely satisfied by their story that they had left the station to stretch their legs and get a drink while waiting for the Rottweil train. While he searched their briefcase, wallets and pockets, they told him to phone the factory at Rottweil. Waiting pensively at a tavern while the officer phoned the factory, the escapers were blissfully relieved when someone confirmed the story! Perhaps whoever had answered the phone had been too busy to check.

Laughing and drinking with a stranger who told them a long incomprehensible story in Flemish, the E.R.A.s soon slipped out of the beer house, down the road and into a wood. Working their way towards the Swiss border by compass they lay up in woods during the day. Early next morning they pulled tiles off the low roof of a woodman's hut in a clearing and dropped inside. Hammond pulled the lock off the door and kept it shut with a piece of string. Lister cut knots out of wood for spy holes. Eating the rest of their food, they waited for dusk. They had a good all-round view in case they had to retreat in a hurry.

A road passed within half a mile of the border. Beyond the road was a marshy field of grass, then fields down to a wood, which was in Switzerland. Leaving five marks under the broken lock the escapers walked off into rising mist. They knew motor-cyclists patrolled the road. Following the railway line west they then tramped south alongside the wood until they heard traffic on the border road. Five miles west of Singen they lay down, checking patrols. They waited as a motor-cycle roared up the road, headlamp flashing. Three minutes later they crossed the road and plunged into the marshy grass. After tramping on for 25 minutes they knew they must almost be in Switzerland. "Halt! Wer Da?" (Halt! Who is there?) The sentry had glimpsed only a dark shadow. While Hammond showed himself in the beam of the torch, the taller Lister crept round the sentry. With Lister rising out of the darkness Hammond suddenly saw moonlight glinting on the Swiss Cross of a greatcoat button. He yelled "No Tubby . . . he's Swiss." Twisting the knife away Lister fell limply against the man. Laughing and joking they identified themselves and waited while the sentry shouted to a fellow soldier. At the village of Ramsden they swallowed hot Army soup then slept soundly under warm blankets. Later they held a great Christmas party with other escapers from Colditz.

The German occupation of southern France in November, 1942, disrupted arrangements for passing Allied escapers. While the E.R.A.s waited in Switzerland the London Gazette of May 11, 1942, announced the award of the British Empire Medal to them both "for bravery and enterprise."

When they finally left Switzerland, they were taken through France by the French Resistance, smuggled over the Pyrenees into Spain, and passed on to Gibraltar. So it was, some four years after leaving their submarine bases, that the two E.R.A.s returned to Britain. Other submariners got back to Britain before them, in exchanges of wounded and disabled prisoners, but Engine Room Artificers Hammond and Lister remain the only British submariners who ever broke out of German prison camps during the second world war and actually got back to Britain.

Pollyanna

When Presidents Reagan and Gorbachev exchanged goodwill gifts at Geneva, two ex-submariners could not help remembering the present they got from the Russians back in 1941 – Pollyanna, the Red Reindeer.

The Cold War may be thawing out a bit now, but Royal Navy submarines are still not exactly welcome up in the Kola inlet. Forty years ago, things were different and the Soviets were happy to play host to any ally in the fight against Nazi Germany. In November, 1941, Petty Officer Jim Riddoch and Torpedoman Bob Swift were at Polyarnoe submarine base in the T-class boat *Trident* when they saw a large sack drop down the forward hatch. Inside was a young reindeer, promptly christened Pollyanna.

It turned out that their captain, Commander Geoffrey Sladen, D.S.O., D.S.C., had mentioned at dinner with a Russian admiral that where his wife lived she had to push a pram up a steep hill. The admiral had a sense of humour. "I'll give you a reindeer to pull it up!" he offered. He meant it, too, and as *Trident* began her long voyage home it occurred to the crew that the Russian's idea of a joke was a bit on the heavy side. As indeed, before long, was the atmosphere inside the submarine.

"It did pong a bit," admits Jim, now 70 and living in Blackburn. "I used to swill it down in the bathroom now and then. The skipper didn't seem to mind – it often used to sleep in his cabin and he would fall over it in the dark. Sometimes it would get between his legs when he was looking through the periscope and he would have to order it out of the control room. 'Riddoch, remove this animal,' he would yell."

It was to Jim, as captain's steward, that the job of "zoo attendant" had fallen. The Russians had provided a sack of moss for fodder but this soon ran out and Pollyanna happily settled for a diet of scraps, washed down with Carnation milk, which she adored. Pollyanna presumably found the smell of 56 unwashed human bodies a little oppressive, too, for whenever the submarine surfaced, her ears pricked up at the sound of the tannoy and she would be first into the control room waiting for the hatch to open.

Trident was required to patrol off Norway before returning home for a much-needed overhaul, and it was six weeks before she finally put into the wartime submarine base at Blyth, near Newcastle-upon-Tyne. Then it was found that Pollyanna had put on weight. Getting her through the hatch was going to be no easy task – but fortunately Torpedoman Bob Swift was a butcher in civilian life. "I knew what to do with calves," says Bob, now 67 and living in Preston. "I secured three of her legs in a sugar bag and she went through with a bit of a push."

Once ashore, Pollyanna soon found her land legs and hared off down the jetty after a couple of dogs, straight past the official from the

Russian Embassy who had been hoping to make some sort of hand-over ceremony. Strangely enough, once she had been caught and brought back to the submarine, Pollyanna seemed reluctant to leave her old home.

Trident survived the war, but by a sad irony both perished within a week of each other five years later, Pollyanna in Regent's Park Zoo and *Trident* in the breaker's yard. It seems she never forgot her career as the Royal Navy's strangest submariner, and Bob still hears stories about her to this day. They say that whenever she heard a bell ring or a sound like a tannoy, she would put her head down just as she used to when preparing for diving stations.